The Album of
ANTHONY POWELL'S
DANCE TO
THE MUSIC OF TIME

The Album of ANTHONY POWELL'S DANCE TO THE MUSIC OF TIME

EDITED BY VIOLET POWELL

PREFACE BY
ANTHONY POWELL

INTRODUCTION BY
JOHN BAYLEY

WITH 224 ILLUSTRATIONS

THAMES AND HUDSON

Printed and bound in Spain by
Artes Gráficas Toledo, S.A.
D.L.T.O.: 385-1987

Contents

'I found myself in the Wallace Collection, standing in front of Nicolas Poussin's picture there given the title *A Dance to the Music of Time*. An almost hypnotic spell seems cast by this masterpiece on the beholder. I knew all at once that Poussin had expressed at least one important aspect of what the novel must be.'

To Keep the Ball Rolling, Chapter 10

Preface

WHEN READING A BOOK I HAVE WRITTEN, in print for the first time, I am always conscious of a sense of surprise. Who is this man who purports to express things which closely resemble what I might have said myself, yet are at the same time somehow unfamiliar? No doubt this same bewilderment is common to most writers.

If that is true of the text of a novel, how much more true of a volume which sets out to portray the visual side of the novelist's mind, the images projected on its screen over a sequence of twelve books. Did I really, directly or indirectly, deal with these landscapes, street scenes, tableaux of figures; allow my imagination to stray over such a disparate miscellany of groups and portraits?

Here we have something rather different from the author's own manuscript set up in print. In the case of this Album other persons have expanded what began in the author's own mind. My wife laid the Album's foundations; other members of the family (including the third generation) contributed to the photography; while the researches of the publisher gave birth to what seem to me sometimes brilliant elaborations of the theme.

The point I make is that, although naturally I offered certain suggestions when the volume was being put together, a few criticisms after it had been assembled, the Album's final impact is as new to me as to anyone else no more than reasonably familiar with the pages of *A Dance to the Music of Time*.

I have always been interested in the consumer end of the Arts, what the reader inevitably adds to the information given by the writer; the way the individual who looks at a picture digests and amplifies what the painter has set down on canvas. In the case of the novelist, readers have often made clear how far they have strayed from my original intention in interpreting the words I have written; not necessarily in an uncreative manner. More than once I have been struck by the power of one's own words to have a life of their own that is separate from oneself.

In this Album it is possible to see illustrated what some of these unexpected side-effects have been. The freshness of much of it to myself brings a profusion of curious feelings. Pictures that form in the mind when writing are never precisely accurate (whether in recollection of events or the composition of actual paintings), still less can be their descriptions when conveyed to others.

It seems to me that an extraordinary richness is reproduced here; a reminder of personal tastes and forgotten sensations; a renewal of strongly felt experiences; sometimes even what Shakespeare calls 'brief abstract and record of tedious days', or Tennyson's 'portions and parcels of the dreadful past,' have developed a kind of beauty of their own.

John Bayley's perceptive Introduction says what is necessary in presenting all that follows. I want to do no more than hint at some of the aspects of the Album that seem to develop advantageously what is to be found in the novel.

Bayley, for instance, makes rather a feature of the story of Candaules and Gyges as depicted on the Tiepolo ceiling of the Venetian Palazzo in *Temporary Kings*. Perhaps I might add a brief note to what he says.

I had always found the relationship of Candaules and Gyges of peculiar fascination. At one moment I planned to attempt a play on the subject, finally deciding somehow to insert the story into a novel. Part of its interest consisted in supposing that, so far as I knew, it had never been used by any of the Old Masters.

After I had introduced the incident into *Dance* I found that, on the contrary, not only had several French painters used Candaules and Gyges as a subject for their brush, but even our own Etty, and that I must have seen the picture by Jordaens reproduced here, when I went round the Gallery in Stockholm not so very many years ago. Somehow it had completely passed from memory, though it came back at once when I saw the photograph.

The Jordaens is in every respect the antithesis of what the Tiepolo would have been. Candaules's Queen, a strapping Netherlands vrow, a Flanders mare if ever there was one, is stepping stark naked over her chamber pot on the way to bed. On the right, low in the picture, two lubricious boors, the King and the Captain of his Guard, peer through a gap in the arras. It is, in fact, the story reduced to its lowest common denominator.

That seems to me why it is arresting. I think the same characteristic attaches to several other of the pictures brought together here, which, a little different from what is suggested in the novel, develop its principle of universality. At least I hope that is so, and that readers may find an expansion of ideas in turning the Album's pages.

ANTHONY POWELL

The Ikon and the Music

THE RELATION BETWEEN FACT AND FICTION is always mysterious. Nowadays academic critics urge us to remember at all times that what we are reading is a fiction, a construct made of words which signify only themselves and refer only to other fictions. This is a rather bleak way of looking at things, as if when watching a film we were only allowed to see it in terms of zoomshots and close-ups and make-up and actors on the set. To most people it is more natural to look at it as life or at least as a story about life.

The same is true of the novel. I once knew a serious lady who was a great admirer of the novelist C. S. Forester and his Hornblower series about the Navy in the time of the Napoleonic wars. After many adventures and vicissitudes Captain Hornblower marries, *en secondes noces,* his true love, Lady Barbara Wellesley, sister of the general who will shortly become the Duke of Wellington. My serious lady was very concerned to find out whether the Duke's sister really did marry a distinguished naval officer. I remarked that if the Duke really did have a sister called Barbara, a point upon which I was in ignorance, it should indeed be possible to find out whom she married. But I hinted at the possibility that the novelist might have made the whole thing up. 'Oh surely not,' the lady replied, 'because for one thing the Duke of Wellington's elder brother comes into one of the novels, and he was a real person – Richard Wellesley.'

I felt inclined to say that people in good novels are real persons, whether they existed in history or not, and that from the reader's point of view they may be more real than any originals in life, existing in history or encountered by the novelist. But it struck me that this might merely confuse the issue. The main thing was that she enjoyed the novels so much, enjoyed them to the extent of believing that the people and events in them must be 'true'. So of course they were, in terms of art: art, in the hands of a master, being cunning enough not only to combine real events and people with made-up ones, but to blur, in various ways, the distinction between the two. I remembered that a distinguished novelist and literary critic, David Lodge, had, in the course of an interesting study of the theory of fiction, issued a rather damping judgment. Discussing Arnold Bennett's novel *The Old Wives' Tale,* he drew attention to the scene in which Sophia, one of the two 'old wives' – youthful and beautiful in the earlier chapters – resolves to take a precaution against the spendthrift nature of the young fellow she has eloped with. While he is sleeping off his hangover in a French hotel she takes the banknotes from his pocket and looks about for a place to hide the other papers she finds there, so that he will think his pocket has been picked. A cupboard suggests itself. 'She got on a chair, and pushed the fragments out of sight on the topmost shelf, where they may well be to this day.' It would be a very foolish reader, comments David Lodge, who would think that those papers really are there, at the top of a cupboard in a hotel in a French provincial town.

Perhaps it would. But it would be an ungenerous reader of novels who did not take for granted the convention to which Arnold Bennett is archly drawing our attention. Why read novels at all unless we, in some sense, believe what they tell us?

The novel which insists that there is no truth in it, and that it is simply an artificial machine devised for our entertainment, is like the film which wants us only to notice how it was shot: both seem to be made only for critics and professional connoisseurs of form.

Anthony Powell is a brilliant master of form. All his novels show that, from *Afternoon Men*, which appeared in 1921, to *The Fisher King*, which came out in 1986. But all his novels are also the most marvellous stories, in which the reader can become absorbed, as if he were himself taking a part in the society described. This is a rare combination, which helps to give his novels, particularly his great *roman fleuve*, their unique status in our time. No other long novel or novel series, not even Proust's *A La Recherche du Temps Perdu*, is based on the same kind of formal principles as *A Dance to the Music of Time*. Proust's principle of construction is indeed very different, more philosophical, more metaphysical even, in a fashion suited to the French intellectual tradition. Whatever the advantages to a sustained narrative of Proust's great metaphysical theory, and they are clearly formidable, his novel does lend itself to undoubted *longueurs* – to whole stretches of ingrowing prose, like much of *La Prisonnière*, which seem of much more absorbing interest to the narrator than they can be to the reader. Marcel's feelings for the captive Albertine are, frankly, a lot less interesting to most readers than would have been more information, more analysis, more *histoires*, about Albertine herself.

If the spool or token from which Proust unwinds his narrative thread is a metaphysical one, Powell's is pictorial. That is obvious. Less obvious, perhaps, are the implications for the pace and tempo of his novel. A dance, such as is performed by the four seasons in Poussin's picture, to the melody supplied by the old gentleman in one corner and the infant in the other, depends on the maintenance of its harmony and the subordination of the participants' inner feelings and reflections to their role in the dance. If the narrator can be considered at once the infant and the greybeard in the picture, he is calling the tune, in the literal sense, but at the same time he is in thrall to the flux and continuity of movement that he is creating. He cannot, so to speak, stop playing and give us an improvisation of his own, while the dancers stand about. The dance may be spontaneous, but it is also collective and interdependent; no individual taking part can halt or step outside it.

But the originality of Powell's method goes much further than this. As befits a novel based on the English rather than the Gallic principle, it takes the form of an anecdote rather than a personal statement or disquisition. And the anecdote is itself the basis of the memoir form. Powell made himself an expert on Aubrey, on whom he wrote an excellent book. Aubrey's *Brief Lives* are jottings to form the basis of a more extended work, a work never completed, or rather never systematically undertaken. Anecdotes no doubt never should be. So that the formal movement and configuration prearranged in a dance pattern are combined, in the atmosphere and feel of the great novel, with the quite different world of the anecdote, which is intimate and unbuttoned, provisional and corroborative, as if a person to person exchange were taking place in which the story-teller spun out his recollections in differing ways, or deferred sometimes to the memories and suggestions of his *tête-à-tête*. Between the figures of a dance and the gestures appropriate to a smoking-room story there might seem to be so big a contrast as to amount to a decided incongruity, but the reader is never conscious of this, except in the sense that such incongruities are part of the general flavour of existence. And pictorial art, too, flourishes on incongruity. Pictures in Powell's novel interweave with the characters, as if all together were taking part in a dance, sometimes a pavane or minuet, sometimes a rout or bucolic kermesse – drunken and jolly, falling and tripping in a booth or fairground, where such an image as that evoked by Horace Isbister's picture *Clergyman eating an Apple* treads a not undiscordant measure with the bronze nymph from the foyer of the Ritz, who looks 'immensely respectable; less provocative, indeed, than some of the fully dressed young women seated below her'; while in the background military attachés merge in drinking and card-playing to form a group (as it happens to be glimpsed at Heathrow) entitled *Boors at an Airport*.

But more effective still than the contrast in alliance between anecdote and picture, formal grouping and informal humour, is the closely related contrast between fiction and reality. Nothing shows the complete originality of Powell's technique more than the way his fiction imitates memoir, and almost in a double sense, like a *trompe l'oeil* painting. The reader, that is to say, quickly grasps that the work is invented, like all novels, and the pictorial element helps him to understand the nature of the invention that is going on. Yet there is deception in this because the work in its own inimitable way *is* a memoir, a memoir masquerading as a novel, an anecdote arranging itself in the elaborate composition of a picture. The two images constantly change and dissolve into each other, so that the reader is happily deceived by the resemblance to reminiscence into supposing that this cannot really be reminiscence at all, but a complicated and inventive story confection, while the notion of a dance, and Poussin's picture of the seasons dancing, artificializes the simple tone proper to the always fascinating discussion about what happened to old so-and-so, and did she ever get married again; if so, to whom?

This mixture – how it is concocted, how received by us – is one of the most fascinating aspects of the novel. But as with all really good novels we ingest it like a drink, a much more alcoholic one than the insipid mixture of 'life' itself, but one to be drunk and enjoyed in the same sort of way. The art, the story, the characters – they all go down together; and it may not be irrelevant that there is a great deal in the novel of what might be called the Arnold Bennett syndrome. He suggested to his readers that some papers secreted by his heroine may still repose at the very top of a tall *armoire* in a small hotel in Auxerre. It increases the reader's sense of fact – the facts the novel deals in; but the facts that Powell provides are much more tangible. There *is* still a bronze nymph, although she has been newly gilded and spring-cleaned, in the foyer of the Ritz hotel. The equestrian statue of Haig, about which there was so much controversy both in reality and in the novel, stands in reality in Whitehall, as it was about to stand in fiction. There really was a general – and a very famous and distinguished one – who used in the war years to run up the steps of the War Office and boom 'Good Morning' at the porters and passers-by. It is true that we should not be able to find a large canvas entitled *Boyhood of Cyrus*, and executed by Edgar Deacon, in any house or gallery at home or abroad; but there is a very similar picture, by Frederick Lord Leighton, and wonderfully absurd it is, even though the real Leighton was a much better painter than the imaginary Deacon, and the narrator would hardly have felt inclined to criticize in his picture – as he does in Deacon's – something unsatisfactory in the foreshortening of the slaveboy's loins.

This unique blend of fact and fiction brings up the whole question of how a novelist – and in particular a novelist of the first rank – invents or creates his characters. It is easy to say that such a novelist has powers of synthesis and adaptation which enable him to pluck a real person out of the air, so to speak, or, as Dickens put it, to sit down and think of Mr Pickwick. It is comparatively easy to produce a character who is recognizably like someone the writer knows in life, and run-of-the-mill novelists do this all the time; but the curious disadvantage to this simple process is that the character so portrayed will seem like neither one thing nor the other – neither a just portrait nor a created fictional character. An example might be Alroy Kear, the leading character in Somerset Maugham's novel *Cakes and Ale*, who is avowedly taken from the real life author Hugh Walpole. Everyone who knew Hugh Walpole – in particular his biographer Rupert Hart-Davis – has testified that he was absolutely unlike Alroy Kear; and at the same time Alroy Kear has no character of his own in the novel other than that attributed by the malice of Maugham to his model. Kear, in short, is a caricature of certain officious traits in Walpole, as a well-known literary busybody, which had aroused Maugham's malignant amusement.

That is one way of doing it, but it will not provide the character bases for a deeply considered work of art. Dostoevsky, in *The Possessed*, portrayed his fellow writer Turgenev as a character called Karmazinov, and any reader at once perceives its falsity, a falsity arising from envy and dislike. There is in fact a sharp contrast in Dostoevsky between such portraits, based on real people, and his true characters – Shatov, the young Verkhovensky, the Underground Man – who, like Mr Pickwick, are in a sense plucked out of the air; who have the most vivid kind of metaphysical existence but one which is no way based on any recognizable traits in an actual individual.

It is such traits which the reader can grasp the truth of in a novel, even though he has no idea where they come from or to what living person they refer. Dickens may have thought of Mr Pickwick, and written a novel which made Pickwick a household word, yet Pickwick has no physical individuality at all: he is a bundle of conventional attributes – benevolence, plumpness, innocence, owlishness, etc. What makes him unique, like P. G. Wodehouse's Jeeves, is what he does and what he stands for, not what he is as a single individual. It might be thought that Powell's Widmerpool, by now as famous a character in the annals of English fiction as either Pickwick or Jeeves, has the same kind of fictional existence as they have, but this is not the case. Widmerpool is built up from a sequence of pictures, vignettes, glimpses, as if done by a series of brilliant artists and photographers. Widmerpool on a misty raw evening in football jersey and running shoes and ill-fitting cap; Widmerpool labouring on the dance floor, as if rowing a small dinghy in a rough sea; Widmerpool drawing in his neck with a slavish expression, as a cascade of sugar unexpectedly voids itself into his hair and collar; Widmerpool observing approvingly, at the frugal supper bestowed on the narrator at his mother's flat: 'You are wearing your bridge coat, mother'.

This series of pictures is also furnished with recordings, so to speak, which give the exact tone of the Widmerpool voice; but the main impression is one of pictures or film-shots (Powell worked in films before the war, and the narrator in *A Dance to the Music of Time*, also working at a film studio, is a keen cinema buff who queues up with his current girl friend to see the classic *Man of Aran*, directed by Robert Flaherty) which flick over before us in rapid succession in a kind of arch or curve, giving the Widmerpool career from childhood to maturity and death. Some critics, but not, I think, readers, have objected to the concept of the dance as being out of keeping with the way in which Powell's characters – and indeed those we meet in life itself – actually present themselves, and see themselves as living out their allotted years. I cannot agree with this objection. The idea of the dance, and the experience of real time, are indeed incongruous with each other, just as art is with life, but it is part of the immense pervasive humour of the novel to bring them together, as they are brought together in the grave and graceful composition of Poussin himself. Humour is not necessarily 'funny': and its range of implication and meaning is as penetrating and delightful in Poussin's canvas as it is in Powell's novel.

So Widmerpool travels from his schooldays to the House of Lords, and on to the nightmare surrealist school of the 'counterculture'. A dance is not a sequential but a circular movement, in and around the same area, and we become gradually aware that, from one point of view, time endlessly repeats itself. The same thought comes briefly to the narrator, Nick Jenkins, in *The Valley of Bones*, when he is discussing at a military exercise near Aldershot the affair that Brent has had with Jenkins's own ex-mistress, Jean Duport. Brent tells Jenkins that Duport refused to believe it when he got wind of his wife's affair – Brent being an absurd figure, not to be thought of as a wife-stealer – until Jean herself 'flew off the handle and told him everything'. Jenkins immediately sees the parallel situation that had occurred during his own affair with Jean, when he had made a slighting remark about an equally absurd character, Jimmy Stripling, and Jean, 'immediately furious', had revealed that he had been a former lover. 'The pattern was, as ever, endlessly repeated.'

Yet the wide spaces of the novel do not emphasise this in any way, just as they do not emphasize the circular progression of Widmerpool himself. The formidableness of the latter, his industry, his capacity for leadership, are never in doubt, and we believe in them absolutely. That in itself is a remarkable achievement on Powell's part, to show how an apparent figure of fun is, in worldly matters, shrewd, responsible, and effective. The 'shots' of Widmerpool at work are just as vivid and authentic as those in which we see his more grotesque side: looking warily round the flat from which his wife Pamela has absconded, leaving the bath tap on; running conscientiously over the school fields as a boy, and then – at the end of his life – running desperately in the nudity favoured by a hippy gang; determined, even in this unlikely context, to get ahead, to show that he can do it better than the others. The instinct of competition, even in the most incongruous or trivial circumstances, is a keynote of Widmerpool's life – though it is far from being the only one – and the pattern of the dance ends for him as it began – 'rowing' on the dance floor, running in his always unsuitable garments, a true and touching antithesis or counterfigure to the graceful quartet that Poussin has set in perpetual motion on his canvas.

In the course of his narrative Nick Jenkins refers once to the fact that human beings are all driven by their own particular furies. Like most such comments in *A Dance to the Music of Time* this is thrown off casually, and the reader only becomes aware of its significance when 'reflecting' (one of Jenkins's favourite activities) on the action at his leisure, or after he has finished reading. Nothing could be a greater contrast than with Proust's method, which is to issue a long and masterly analysis of, say, jealousy, or the chimerical nature of love, while occasionally referring to human examples. In Powell the picture comes first, with the 'moral' not exactly an afterthought on the part of the writer but a kind of dawning realization which he has inserted in the reader's mind. Thus Widmerpool is a premier example of a man pursued by furies, but what are these furies exactly? Suitably enough, they have no bodily substance, and they cannot be portrayed in a picture or photographed by a lens. Widmerpool, running through the marshy mists at school, or – fifty years later – through the woods at his own country home, now given over to the hippy movement and Scorp Murtlock, its charismatic leader – Widmerpool cannot see them and nor can we. But after the book is closed we come to realize the sense in which they were there, and it may make us shiver a little. And laugh again too, for what can be more movingly ludicrous than a man in late middle age still stubbornly competing, as if he was a schoolboy, in an activity in which he had never managed to score any success. All the real success which he has earned is no use to him: he longs only for the kind he can't have, and which came with such effortless ease alike to the gilded youth of his distant schooldays, and to Murtlock as the youthfully sinister portent and representative of the modern age.

The hero of Lermontov's novel *A Hero of Our Time*, which Powell in his time has much admired, is made out of pictures in a manner that is basically very similar to the construction of many memorable figures in *A Dance to the Music of Time*. Pamela Widmerpool is in this respect particularly close to Lermontov's man, Pechorin, who is pursued by furies whom the reader not only never sees but whose significance he cannot fully understand, or even guess at. In this sense the picture that does not tell a story is as effective as the one that does. Tolstoy, himself a great admirer and to some extent an imitator of Lermontov (witness the character of Dolokhov in *War and Peace*), is a great user of the picture method, although he employs it in an interestingly different way, identifying his *dramatis personae* not in scenes or 'shots' but by physical signs and markings, like the dark down on the upper lip of the Little Princess, or the red hairs on the back of Dolokhov's large hands.

Tolstoy himself remarked to a friend that all the characters in his novels could be traced in some way to a real-life original, adding that he did not see how a person described in fiction could appear convincing if this were not so. Tolstoy, as so often, goes to the heart of the matter, incidentally rebutting in his downright way the notion treasured in certain critical circles – circles in which novels don't actually get written – that in superior fiction people from life don't intrude, having in some way been metamorphosed into wholly fictional creation. In nine cases out of ten Tolstoy is surely right; Mr Pickwick may have no original in life but Anna Karenina and Natasha Rostov most certainly have, and if there were no flesh and blood individuals behind them – individuals whom Tolstoy had *taken in* as a writer can – they would not be the characters they are. This must *a fortiori* be true of a work of art like Powell's, in which the relation between novel and memoir, the invented and the recalled, is so subtly and comprehensively interwoven.

I must return in a moment to this important question, one on which Anthony Powell himself has written perceptively in his memoirs, but let us for the moment follow up, in connection with the pictorial ambiance of *A Dance to the Music of Time*, the ways in which the physical iconography, as it were, of real people finds its way into Powell's memorable portraits. All such portraits are composite in one sense – that is to say, the physical characteristics of several different persons may be reassembled, among the dancers, as those belonging to a single individual. And this produces incongruity of the most fruitful and delightful sort, of the same kind indeed that exists between the aesthetic notion of time as a dance, and the quotidian experience of it as a sandstorm or accumulation, beating us in, as Philip Larkin puts it, with 'the blows of what happened to happen'; the time that creates Arnold Bennett's 'tragedy in ten thousand acts' in *The Old Wives' Tale*. In the course of the dance we look quite different, when the next picture or snapshot of us is taken. Appearances change; new physical tokens and hallmarks replace the old. And this curiosity of time's operation is inconspicuously conveyed by Powell again and again, so that we hardly notice it except as part of the rich collective impression.

It may be, as so often happens with very good novelists, that what began as a *curiosa felicitas*, an accidental scoring of effect, may then have become for the writer a technique, even if a technique which in its very nature cannot be pursued with full consciousness. But like all the best literary techniques this one immeasurably enhances the 'felt life', as Henry James would say, in the novel series. Take the successive pictures of Stringham, or of Dicky Umfraville. Both, like most of the dancers, are clearly composite portraits, with something taken from one person in Powell's life and something from another. A single original no doubt predominates – that of Hubert Duggan in the case of Stringham, as we know from *Infants of the Spring*, the first volume of Powell's memoirs: possibly Basil Hamborough, a friend of a later period, in the case of Umfraville. From the standpoint of art, however, what is significant is that nuances of behaviour from several people can be coalesced into those of one, so as to give the impression that they have changed with time: and those changes are something we can all identify and recognize.

Thus Umfraville in his later metamorphoses is far from being the 'purely nocturnal creature' whom he rallies Nick Jenkins on supposing him to be, when they next meet after a previous encounter at the night club Umfraville happens to be running. And in his last avatar he has lost that 'not entirely sane' look which Jenkins notices in the war, when he meets the Umfraville who has just got engaged to his sister-in-law Frederica. Stringham has a look of the young Alexander in Veronese's picture in the National Gallery (page 31) – a point we can now confirm from the portrait on the same page of Hubert Duggan with his stepfather, Lord Curzon. Curzon himself hovers briefly in the middle ground of the dance when we meet Buster Foxe, Stringham's stepfather, at the house of his mother, with its 'doublefronted façade in a small street near Berkeley Square: the pillars of the entrance flanked on either side with hollow cones for the linkmen to extinguish their torches'. Buster 'diffused waves of personality, strong, chilling gusts of icy air, a protective element that threatened to freeze into rigidity all who came through the door, before they could approach him nearer'.

This, by all accounts, would be an excellent description of the impression made by Curzon himself, but it is also exactly the feeling that a rather over-awed youth up from school might have in the presence of Buster. When Jenkins is grown-up, a seasoned Londoner, Buster will seem quite different, as he does at the party for Hugh Moreland, and the difference is probably attributable to the fact that another real-life original from Powell's own collection of 'Brief Lives' can be glimpsed in the background. The process works particularly well in the case of Sillery, the worldly don and later Labour peer whom Jenkins first encounters at Oxford. We know from the Powell memoirs that Sillery is a composite portrait, to some extent based on two notable dons of the period, 'Sligger' Urquhart at Balliol, and Maurice Bowra of

Wadham, then a much younger man, not long launched on a career of fame and influence. (It should be added that Cambridge sources utterly deny the resemblance of Sillery to Urquhart and Bowra, suggesting that, on the contrary, Sillery far more closely reflects the characteristics of Ernest Barker, a don Powell encountered during a wartime army course at Cambridge.) Of course Sillery remains an imaginary embodiment of certain don-like characteristics carried to their apotheosis, after the fashion of High Renaissance portraiture, in which Powell obviously delights. 'Sligger' Urquhart did however run a salon much like the one Nick Jenkins attends for tea and rock-buns during his first term, presided over by Sillery; and while Sillery in no way resembles Bowra physically he makes certain gestures, brilliantly caught by Powell, which leave no doubt about a resemblance to his celebrated original. Here he is attending a lunch party given by Stringham.

> Stringham offered him sherry, which was refused. Like many persons more interested in power than sensual enjoyment, Sillery touched no strong drink. Prowling about the room for a moment or two, he glanced at the invitations on the mantelpiece: a London dance or two, and some undergraduate parties. He found nothing there that appeared to interest him, because he turned, and, stepping between Stringham and myself, took each of us by an arm, resting his weight slightly.

The gesture of catching two persons simultaneously by the arm is unmistakable, as is the action – Bowra having practically no neck – of turning himself bodily towards anyone he spoke to, a gesture caught by Elizabeth Bowen and assigned to a somewhat Bowra-like character in her novel *To the North*. But when we last meet Sillery in *A Dance to the Music of Time* such physical characteristics and gestures seem to belong to a distant past. Time has not diminished his physical sprightliness, but has transformed it into ape-like movements, such as the leap into a squatting position that he makes while searching in a low cupboard for the manuscript volume of his memoirs. It is significant too that Sillery on this occasion is having a mild flirtation, almost a love affair, with the pretty secretary, Ada Leintwardine, who is helping him edit his memoirs: a further unemphatic, almost invisible, indication of the important truth that even those who have almost reached the end of their dance measure to time are by no means immune to the excitements and disappointments of love.

All novels depend to a great extent upon our entering with the author into what might be called an 'understanding' relationship. We must have some means of communication with himself and his world, that is to say, which seems unique to it and to what it offers. Tolstoy, in his autobiographical *Childhood, Boyhood and Youth*, remarks that a great deal depends, especially when we are young, on the friendships we form with others with whom we have a sort of mutual pact of 'understanding', of grasping, in terms of our mutual knowledge or ignorance, what the world is all about. With people who seem to lack such a mode of understanding we may be very friendly but cannot really be closely intimate. With Nick Jenkins and his world of time's music we must have such an understanding; and it merges insensibly into the way in which Jenkins himself feels in relation to some people he meets and not others. Though not much interested in music as such he has an especially understanding relation with Hugh Moreland, as Powell himself had with Constant Lambert (see volume three of the Memoirs, *Faces in My Time*). In a quite different way Jenkins also acquires it with the members of a large family, the Tollands, by the process of himself becoming a member of the family through marriage. There is thus a subtle linkage between our 'understanding' of the great novel and its author and narrator's understanding of his life and surroundings through this kind of relation with the family, as with other friends. Powell himself has written most perceptively about this in *Faces in My Time*.

It has been suggested (by a member of the Pakenham family belonging to a younger generation than my own, who at the same time agreed not even approximate individual portraits existed) that the general tone of the Tollands in facing life is not unlike that of the Pakenhams. Such a possibility is something of which I cannot be sure (novelists possessing less conscious control of what they write than is supposed), and the comment may well be true. Indeed, it would be surprising were no similarity at all observable. In one particular case I would go further, conceding that in Isobel Tolland faint nuances (of which I am myself probably unaware) may to some extent mark her out as my wife; part of that autonomous side of writing which can carry more conviction than careful thought on the part of an author.

'The general tone of the Tollands in facing life' is an indication worth considering carefully. It could suggest the individual style in facing the portrait painter, or the camera; as if 'facing life' were, in terms of the formal structure of the novel, a process analogous to being rendered as a part of it. The idea of living life with style of course suggests the High Renaissance idea of living life as if one were part of a formal composition – a family group as it might be – or at least in accordance with an aesthetic and pictorial ideal. It would be tempting to conclude that the iconographical key to *A Dance to the Music of Time* is to be found in the Tolland family itself, as if Poussin's dancing group were a selection of them doing a little number as part of that extravagant delight in dressing up and having a show which Jenkins notes as characteristic of such old families. But this would none the less be misleading. Truer to say, perhaps, that while all the characters begin as 'dancers', in some sense, they then reveal themselves more fully, and often more surprisingly, in relation to each other, to their personal furies, and to Jenkins himself.

The pictorial method is strikingly successful in giving us the image or ikon of a new character, which will then expand, change, and transform itself as we get to know the person better. Members and Quiggin, for instance, are introduced to us at a Sillery tea-party in *A Question of Upbringing*, like two unrelated totem figures. They are sitting at opposite ends of a sofa, and, in order to express his repugnance for his neighbour, 'Members brought his knees right up to his chin, clasping his hands round them in the position shown in a picture (that used to hang in the nursery of a furnished house we had once inhabited in Colchester) called The Boyhood of Raleigh.' Iconographically speaking, all boyhoods have something in common. Raleigh, the great king Cyrus, and other heroic figures – they all share the need to grow up somehow: all are figures in the ironic comedy which might be titled 'A Question of Upbringing'. Piqued by his contiguity with Quiggin, Members rises from the floor and casts himself 'almost full length on the floor in front of the fireplace: exchanging in this manner his Boyhood-of-Raleigh posture for that of the Dying Gladiator'.

Quiggin and Members will appear later in quite different guises, and even here their association makes a point – like so many in the novel – of peculiar historical interest; an interest, that is to say, which performs the dual function of illuminating not only the general action and outlook of the novel but the more impersonal world outside it. (In the same way a true memoir is interesting both for itself and for the light it throws on the manners of its age.) Quiggin and Members, so apparently different in style and outlook, are revealed, in the circumstances of Sillery's tea-party, to have the same background, even to live practically in the same street in the same town. This not only underlines the form and structure which sustains the whole fiction – lives that seem so separate are in reality constantly intermingling – but serves to exhibit the unfamiliar but very significant social point that choice of style in the individual is always very much more than just a matter of class background. Within limits we can decide ourselves what impression we want to make; and this was particularly true of the University circles of the twenties and thirties in which different classes and lifestyles were being increasingly mixed up. Members opted for the upwardly mobile image of young poet, aesthete, fashionable Oxford type: Quiggin for the new proletarian stance, uncouth, minatory, no-nonsense. Both, in practice, are on the make in the same way, using the same weapons and the same social contacts; and both will turn out to succeed in life in the same field, neither being handicapped by any real political or social convictions.

Sometimes, of course, the preliminary ikon is all we need in order to fix a character in his place in the book. In the enormously comical but deadly accurate military sequences, figures suddenly reveal their identities in terms of some other and equally hierarchic system of iconography, like the two colonels and the major-general at the Divisional Headquarters where Jenkins is serving in the lowly capacity of defence platoon commander in *The Soldier's Art*.

Hardy told a friend that the idea of *Tess of the D'Urbevilles* came to him when he briefly glimpsed a handsome waitress in a Weymouth tea-shop. The rest was a matter of day-dreaming on his part, his heroine responding, as it were, to every need and suggestion of his own imaginative life. Although the glimpse is all that is required for Powell, too, to fix a character in a memorable iconographic stance, it is very noticeable that he never *dreams* about his characters as more self-indulgent novelists do, however curiously he may reflect on them. There are also unobtrusive indications that he is aware of the possible weaknesses – in certain circumstances – of the iconographic approach, referring them to shortcomings, perhaps youthful ones, in Jenkins's own view of life. This is exemplified by one of the vignettes of Uncle Giles, who suddenly materializes in Shepherd's Market at four in the morning, when Jenkins is returning from a party.

> I reached the outskirts of Shepherd's Market. . . . Touched, almost mystically, like another Stonehenge, by the first rays of the morning sun, the spot seemed one of those clusters of tumbledown dwellings depicted by Canaletto or Piranesi, habitations from amongst which arches, obelisks and viaducts, ruined and overgrown with ivy, arise from the mean houses huddled together below them. . . . As I penetrated farther into the heart of that rookery, in the direction of my own door, there even stood, as if waiting to greet a friend, one of those indeterminate figures that occur so frequently in the pictures of the kind suggested – Hubert Robert or Pannini – in which the architectural subject predominates. . . . He leant a little to one side on a rolled umbrella, just as those single figures in romantic landscape are apt to pose; as if the painter, in dealing with so much static matter, were determined to emphasise 'movement' in the almost infinitesimal human side of his composition.

This apparition turns out to be Uncle Giles, just up from Surrey, or so he says. The whole passage is a marvellous evocation of a place, a time and a person; and one must notice the scrupulous leisure with which Uncle Giles's conversation (if that is the word) is recorded, and contrast the accuracy establishing his unique individuality with the purely pictorial phenomenon of his presence. After saying goodbye Jenkins prepares for bed.

> While I undressed I reflected on the difficulty of believing in the existence of certain human beings, my uncle among them, even in the face of unquestionable evidence – indications sometimes even wanting in the case of persons for some reason more substantial to the mind – that each had dreams and desires like other men. Was it possible to take Uncle Giles seriously? And yet he was, no doubt, serious enough to himself. If a clue to that problem could be found, other mysteries of life might be revealed. I was still pondering Uncle Giles and his ways when I dropped into an uneasy sleep.

In terms of his iconographical, as of his conversational, personality it is not possible to take Uncle Giles 'seriously'; but through the medium of his, at this stage, callow narrator the author filters to the reader a strikingly different background sense of Uncle Giles as himself, a sense only discernible because the foreground is so immaculately filled with Uncle Giles's conversational humour, and with his aesthetic place in the composition of a landscape and townscape. The humanity of Uncle Giles is all the more poignant through the circumstances in which he is presented, and his final avatar in a south coast hotel is one of the most moving things in a book which is full of feats of this kind, and of scenes as superbly and humorously demonstrative as this Shepherd's Market encounter in the small hours.

It seems possible that Powell intends certain of his characters to remain opaque, and that when this happens their pictorial background, the 'Book of Hours' as it were, is not so brilliantly filled in. Things become more expressionist, like a German film of the 1920s, perhaps *The Cabinet of Dr Caligari*, or like that strangely sinister lay figure, an artist's jointed model, which Misha Black used so effectively for the jackets of Powell's pre-war novels. High Renaissance is suddenly brought face to face and contrasted with an aesthetic of a quite different sort. The incongruity between Tiepolo and the world of Pamela Widmerpool is clearly brought out, illustrating a point of general importance in the novel: that the world of art is closed to those who take themselves and their obsessions too seriously. The charm and variety of the legend, the ebullient splendour of the Tiepolo ceiling, is lost on Pamela, who can see in it one thing only, the one thing that concerns herself. In addition to her other defects as a human being Pamela is the archetypal philistine.

Glober, for all his shortcomings, has genuine aesthetic curiosity, and the liveliness that goes with it. He is open to the impact of art: Pamela is not. And true eroticism goes with the situations in which art feels most at home, as Powell brings out in his comments on the real frescoes by Tiepolo in the Palazzo Labia, which illustrate Antony and Cleopatra's first meeting, and their subsequent banquet.

> These scenes are represented as if taking place in an area beyond the room in which the onlooker stands, each fresco placed between real doors, three marble steps below painted in perspective, as if leading up into a magical land of Egypt. The first shows a courtyard or quay where Cleopatra has been waiting to greet Antony on disembarkation from the ship which has brought him to her realm: the second, a pillared hall, in the foreground of

which the Egyptian Queen – a glorious Venetian beauty – entertains Antony (still wearing his helmet, no doubt to set himself off to best advantage) to dinner. . . .

Among the surrounding retinue – which includes a Beardsleyan dwarf and a small dog disporting themselves on the steps – The Banquet offers one of those self-portraits Tiepolo would sometimes insert in his works. Clad in a robe, the painter stands in the background, watching the proceedings rather sardonically.

In the two Labia frescoes, more especially the scene at the dinner table, the suggestion of mutual sexual expectancy on the faces of Antony and Cleopatra is marvellously conveyed.

Pamela Widmerpool, we may say, has not entered this enchanted world of art, the representation of the music of time in which each panel or fresco is placed in the context of real events, lively characters, a living narrator, who, concealed as himself, stands in the background of his scenes and watches the proceedings, not indeed sardonically, but with quiet gusto and meditative appreciation. It is one of the master-strokes of the oeuvre that a character like Pamela, not accessible to the forms and processes of art which determine the whole, should remain outside, a black spot extraneous to the composition, bringing disaster on all – her husband Widmerpool, Louis Glober, X. Trapnel – who for one reason or another find themselves a part of the swirling forms and draperies of the picture, taking part in the dance.

The perfect contrast with Pamela would be such a figure as General Liddament, the hero of one of the most matchless sequences in the whole novel, and worth quoting because it so perfectly illustrates the ways in which truth, humour, and the pictorial art meld together in its scenes. Liddament, like Pamela, has all the marks of an obsessed and obsessive person, but the philistinism which excludes her from the dance is replaced in his case by a magical embodiment of style, perception, acuity, both subjective and objective, conferred on him by the perception of the narrator, but also brought by himself to add to the grace and gaiety of the measure.

> Though regarded by regular soldiers as something of a military pedant – so Maelgwyn-Jones had told Gwatkin – General Liddament was said to be an officer with ideas of his own. Possibly in order to counteract this reputation for an excessive precision in approach to his duties, an imperfection of which he was probably aware and hoped to correct, the General allowed himself certain informalities of dress and turn-out. For example, he carried a long stick, like the wand of a verger in a cathedral, and wore a black-and-brown check scarf thrown carelessly about his neck. A hunting horn was thrust between the buttons of his battle-dress blouse. Maelgwyn-Jones also reported that two small dogs on a lead sometimes accompanied General Liddament, causing great disturbance when they squabbled with each other. Today must have been too serious an occasion for these animals to be with him. The presence of dogs would have increased his air of being a shepherd or huntsman, timeless in conception, depicted in the idealized pastoral scene of some engraving. However, General Liddament's manner of speaking had none of this mild, bucolic tone.
>
> 'Tell them to carry on,' he said, pointing his long stick at me. 'What's the name of this officer?'
>
> 'Second-lieutenant Jenkins, sir,' said Gwatkin, who was under great strain.
>
> 'How long have you been with this unit, Jenkins?'
>
> I told the General, who nodded. He asked some further questions. Then he turned away, as if he had lost all interest in me, all interest in human beings at all, and began

rummaging furiously about the place with his stick. After exploring the corners of the barn, he set about poking at the roof.

'Have your men been dry here?'

'Yes, sir.'

'Are you sure?'

'Yes, sir.'

'There is a leak in the thatch here.'

'There is a leak in that corner, sir, but the men slept the other end.'

The General, deep in thought, continued his prodding for some seconds without visible effect. Then, as he put renewed energy into the thrusts of his stick, which penetrated far into the roofing, a large piece of under-thatch all at once descended from above, narrowly missing General Liddament himself, completely overwhelming his ADC with debris of dust, twigs and loam. At that, the General abandoned his activities, as if at last satisfied. Neither he nor anyone else made any comment, nor was any amusement expressed. The ADC, a pink-faced young man, blushed hotly and set about cleaning himself up. The General turned to me again.

'What did your men have for breakfast, Jenkins?'

'Liver, sir.'

I was impressed by his retention of my name.

'What else?'

'Jam, sir.'

'What else?'

'Bread, sir – and margarine.'

'Porridge?'

'No, sir.'

'Why not?'

'No issue, sir.'

The General turned savagely on Gwatkin, who had fallen into a kind of trance, but now started agonisingly to life again.

'No porridge?'

'No porridge, sir.'

General Liddament pondered this assertion for some seconds in resentful silence. He seemed to be considering porridge in all its aspects, bad as well as good. At last he came out with an unequivocal moral judgment.

'There ought to be porridge,' he said.

He glared round at the platoon, hard at work with their polishing, oiling; pulling-through, whatever they were doing. Suddenly he pointed his stick at Williams, W. H., the platoon runner.

'Would you have liked porridge?'

Williams, W. H., came to attention. As I have said, Williams, W. H., was good on his feet and sang well. Otherwise, he was not particularly bright.

'No, sir,' he said instantly, as if that must be the right answer.

The General was taken aback. It would not be too much to say he was absolutely staggered.

'Why not?'

General Liddament spoke sharply, but seriously, as if some excuse like religious scruple about eating porridge would certainly be accepted as valid.

'Don't like it, sir.'

'*You don't like porridge?*'

'No, sir.'

'Then you're a foolish fellow – a very foolish fellow.'

After saying that, the General stood in silence, as if in great distress of mind, holding his long staff at arm's length from him, while he ground it deep into the earthy surface of the barnhouse floor. He appeared to be trying to contemplate as objectively as possible the concept of being so totally excluded from the human family as to dislike porridge. His physical attitude suggested a holy man doing penance vicariously for the sin of those in his spiritual care. All at once he turned to the man next to Williams, W. H., who happened to be Sayce.

'Do *you* like porridge?' he almost shouted.

Sayce's face, obstinate, dishonest, covered with pockmarks showed determination to make trouble if possible, at the same time uncertainty as how best to achieve that object. For about half a minute Sayce turned over in his mind the pros and cons of porridge eating, just as he might reflect on the particular excuse most effective in extenuation of a dirty rifle barrel. Then he spoke.

'Well, sir –' he began.

General Liddament abandoned Sayce immediately for Jones, D.

'–and you?'

'No, sir,' said Jones, D., also speaking with absolute assurance that a negative answer was expected of him.

'–and you?'

'No, sir,' said Rees.

Moving the long stick with feverish speed, as if he were smelling out witches, the General pointed successively at Davies, J., Davies, E., Ellis, Clements, Williams, G.

No one had time to answer. There was a long pause at the end of the line. Corporal Gwylt stood there. He had been supervising the cleaning of the bren. General Liddament, whose features had taken on an expression of resignation, stood now leaning forward, resting his chin on the top of the stick, his head looking like a strange, rather malignant totem at the apex of a pole. He fixed his eyes on Gwylt's cap badge, as if ruminating on the history of the Regiment symbolized in the emblems of its design.

'And you, Corporal,' he asked, this time quite quietly. 'Do you like porridge?'

An enormous smile spread over Corporal Gwylt's face.

'Oh, yes, yes, sir,' he said, 'I do like porridge. I did just wish we had had porridge this morning.'

Slowly General Liddament straightened himself. He raised the stick so that its sharp metal point almost touched the face of Corporal Gwylt.

'Look,' he said, 'look, all of you. He may not be the biggest man in the Division, but he is a sturdy fellow, a good type. There is a man who eats porridge. Some of you would do well to follow his example.'

With these words, the Divisional Commander strode out of the barn. He was followed by Gwatkin and the ADC, the last still covered from head to foot with thatch. They picked their way through the mud towards the General's car. A minute later, the pennon disappeared from sight. The inspection was over.

The inspection may be over, as in time the dance itself will have to end, but as Anthony Powell directs them who would miss either?

THE ALBUM

A Dance
to the Music
of Time

A TITLE – AND A THEME. *As day draws in, snow falls gently from a dull sky onto a brazier around which workmen are gathered. Nicholas Jenkins begins a narrative which is to take him and the hundreds of men and women whom he meets and knows through fifty years of English life from the 1920s to the beginning of the 1970s.*

Something in the physical attitudes of the men themselves as they turned from the fire, suddenly suggested Poussin's scene in which the Seasons, hand in hand and facing outward, tread in rhythm to the notes of the lyre that the winged and naked greybeard plays. The image of Time brought thoughts of mortality: of human beings, facing outward like the Seasons, moving hand in hand in intricate measure: stepping slowly, methodically, sometimes a trifle awkwardly, in evolutions that take recognisable shape: or breaking into seemingly meaningless gyrations, while partners disappear only to reappear again, once more giving pattern to the spectacle: unable to control the melody, unable, perhaps, to control the steps of the dance.

Poussin's painting (in the Wallace Collection, London) is the presiding ikon of the whole sequence of novels. Nicholas himself stands apart, sometimes joining in the dance, more often observing the motions of the others as they come together, join hands for a while and part, while the music of Time leads them imperceptibly towards death.

School: the first partners

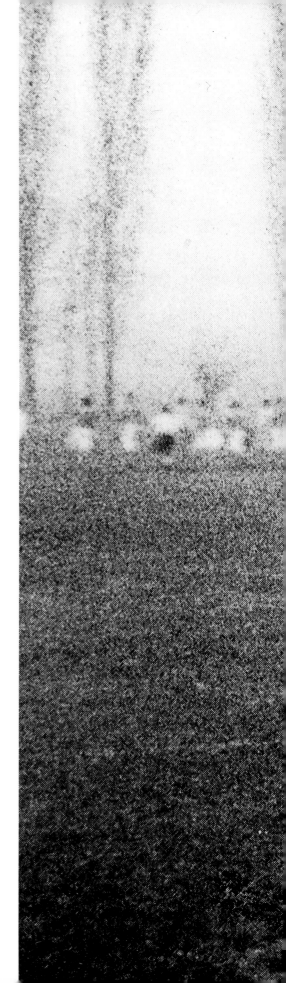

A S WINTER ADVANCED in that river valley, mist used to rise in late afternoon and spread over the flooded grass; until the house and all the outskirts of the town were enveloped in opaque, chilly vapour, tinted like cigar-smoke.

From this mist, at the very beginning of the story, emerges the figure of Widmerpool, in a sweater once white and a cap at least a size too small, hobbling unevenly, though with determination, on the flat heels of spiked running shoes.

Nicholas is at school, one of the older public schools, commanding and antiquated, laid out in a quadrilateral, though irregular, style. Silted-up residues of the years smouldered uninterruptedly – and not without melancholy – in the maroon brickwork of these medieval closes: beyond the cobbles and archway of which (in a more northerly direction) memory also brooded, no less enigmatic and inconsolable, among water-meadows and avenues of trees. *The school is a tight community where esteem is to be won through sport or through precocious knowledge of the world. Widmerpool – dogged, serious and graceless – is so far a failure in both.*

On the threshold

CAPT. BECHER on VIVIAN.

NICHOLAS JENKINS, *Peter Templer and Charles Stringham form a little coterie of boys on the brink of manhood, their preoccupations already centring on the adult world. Stringham's room* contained two late eighteenth-century coloured prints of racehorses. (The previous summer, Stringham and Templer had managed to attend a race-meeting together one half-holiday afternoon without being caught.) *Here Stringham and Templer sit, cook sausages and talk, and the young Nicholas listens with silent attention. Stringham is the more urbane and witty –* [they] argued as we went along about the age of the Dolly Sisters, one of whom Stringham held to be the mother of the other. *But Templer has gone further in the ways of the world.* He had a thin face and light blue eyes that gave out a perpetual and quite mechanical sparkle: at first engaging: then irritating. 'My dear Peter,' *says Stringham,* 'why do you always go about dressed as if you were going to dance up and down a row of naked ladies singing "Dapper Dan was a very handy man", or something equally lyrical? You get more like an advertisement for gents' tailoring every day.'

When we meet Templer he has just come back from London.

'The reason I took the later train was because I was with a girl . . . .'

'Where did you meet her?'

'In the street.'

'Do you mean you picked her up?'

'Yes.'

'Fair or dark?'

'Fair.'

'And how was the introduction effected?'

'She smiled at me.'

'A tart, in other words.'

Stringham: living for the moment

HE WAS TALL AND DARK, and looked a little like one of those stiff, sad young men in ruffs, whose long legs take up so much room in sixteenth-century portraits: or perhaps a younger – and far slighter – version of Veronese's Alexander receiving the children of Darius after the battle of Issus: with the same high forehead and suggestion of hair thinning a bit at the temples. His features certainly seemed to belong to that epoch of painting: the faces in Elizabethan miniatures, lively, obstinate, generous, not very happy, and quite relentless.

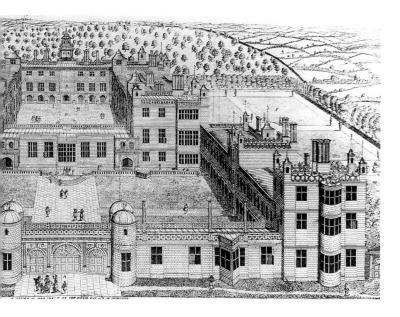

Veronese's Alexander, in the National Gallery, London, himself bore a striking resemblance to Charles Stringham's real-life physical model: Hubert Duggan. Duggan (seen here in hunting clothes with his stepfather Lord Curzon – once perhaps the most magnificent of all Viceroys of India) had 'wit, a strong vein of melancholy, a kind of natural dash and elegance, altogether untouched with "showing off"'.

Stringham is a strong influence on Jenkins in their school days in the early 1920s. Heir to a South African fortune through his mother, he has in his rooms at school an engraving in the manner of Wenceslas Hollar of Glimber, the huge seventeenth-century mansion she inherited from her first husband, the Earl of Warrington.

All the auguries point to a dazzling future for Stringham: he is the wittiest and most charming of Nicholas's early friends (though significantly 'he suffered from prolonged fits of melancholy'), as Widmerpool is the most gauche. But, keenly relishing each moment, he completely lacks Widmerpool's 'quest for power', his wry humour extracting as much enjoyment from failure as from success.

'A beauty and an heiress'

STRINGHAM'S MOTHER, *Mrs Foxe, gives Nicholas his first taste of real elegance when he is taken to lunch at her house on the first day of the holidays after leaving school.* It was a rather gloomy double-fronted façade in a small street near Berkeley Square: the pillars of the entrance flanked on either side with hollow cones for the linkmen to extinguish their torches . . . I followed up the stairs into a room on the first floor, generally crimson in effect, containing a couple of large Regency bookcases. A female portrait, by appearance a Romney, hung over the fireplace, and there was a malachite urn of immense size on a marble-topped table by the window: presented, I learnt later, by the Tsar to one of the Warringtons who had headed some diplomatic mission to Russia at the beginning of the nineteenth century . . . A moment or two later his mother appeared. I thought her tremendously beautiful: though smaller than the photograph in Stringham's room had suggested. Still wearing a hat, she had just come into the house.

Over lunch Nicholas mentions his family.

'I know all about the army,' she said. 'My first husband was a soldier. That was ages ago, of course. Even apart from that we had a house on the Curragh, because he used to train his horses there – so that nothing about soldiering is a mystery to me.'

There was something curiously overpowering about her. Now she seemed to have attached the army to herself, like a piece of property rediscovered after lying for long years forgotten. Lord Warrington had, it appeared, commanded a cavalry brigade before he retired. She told stories of the Duke of Cambridge, and talked of Kitchener and his collection of china.

'Are you going to be a soldier too?' she asked.

'No.'

'I think Charles ought. Anyway for a time. But he doesn't seem awfully keen.'

'No,' said Stringham, 'he doesn't.'

Meeting Buster

'WHO is Buster?'

'My mother's current husband.'

I knew nothing of this figure, except that he was called Lieutenant-Commander Foxe, and that Stringham had once described him as a 'polo-playing sailor'.

Tall, distinguished and handsome, he nevertheless 'had a way of making one feel remarkably ill at ease.' Stringham dislikes him intensely, and when Nicholas sees them together their veiled hostility is evident.

'Aren't you lunching here?' said Stringham.

'I am trying to buy a Bentley from a man awfully cheap. I've got to keep him sweet.'

'Did you sell the Isotta?'

'I had to.'

Buster smiled a little sadly, as if in half public acknowledgment that he himself had long since seen through any illusions once possessed regarding the extent of his wife's fortune; but indicating by the same smile that he had learnt how to bear disappointment. Stringham said: 'Where are you taking him?'

'Claridge's.'

'Will you ply him with drink?'

'Hock, I think. That is what I am feeling like myself. Are you coming to the Russian Ballet tonight?'

'I didn't know I was asked,' Stringham said. 'I'd like to.'

'Do.'

'Anyone for lunch?'

'Only Tuffy. She will be glad to see you.'

'Then we will wish you good luck with your deal.'

I was conscious that some sort of a duel had been taking place, and that Stringham had somehow gained an advantage by, as it were, ordering Buster from the room . . .

As we sat down, Stringham said: 'I hear we are going to the Russian Ballet tonight.'

'It was Buster's idea. He thought you would like it.'

'That was kind of him.'

PERFECTI
BENTLEY CI
BARKER COAC

ALHAMBRA

A visit to the Templers

AT FIRST SIGHT the Templers' house seemed to be an enormously swollen villa, red and gabled, facing the sea from a small park of Scotch firs. . . . The clouded horizon and olive-green waves lapping against the stones made it a place of mystery in spite of this outwardly banal appearance: a sea-palace for a version of one of those embarkation scenes of Claude Lorraine – the Queen of Sheba, St Ursula, or perhaps The Enchanted Castle – where any adventure might be expected.

And indeed it is here that Nicholas first meets Peter's sister Jean. Fair, not strikingly pretty, with long legs and short, untidy hair, she remained without moving, intently watching us . . . her face was thin and attenuated, the whole appearance given the effect of a much simplified – and somewhat selfconscious – arrangement of lines and planes, such as might be found in an Old Master drawing, Flemish or German perhaps, depicting some young and virginal saint; the racquet, held awkwardly at an angle to her body, suggesting at the same time an obscure implement associated with martyrdom. The expression of her face, although sad and a trifle ironical, was not altogether in keeping with this air of belonging to another and better world. I felt suddenly uneasy, and also interested: a desire to be with her, and at the same time, an almost paralysing disquiet at her presence.

Jean, however, betrays no interest in the shy young Nicholas, and it is not until several years later that his feelings for her are reborn in the adult world.

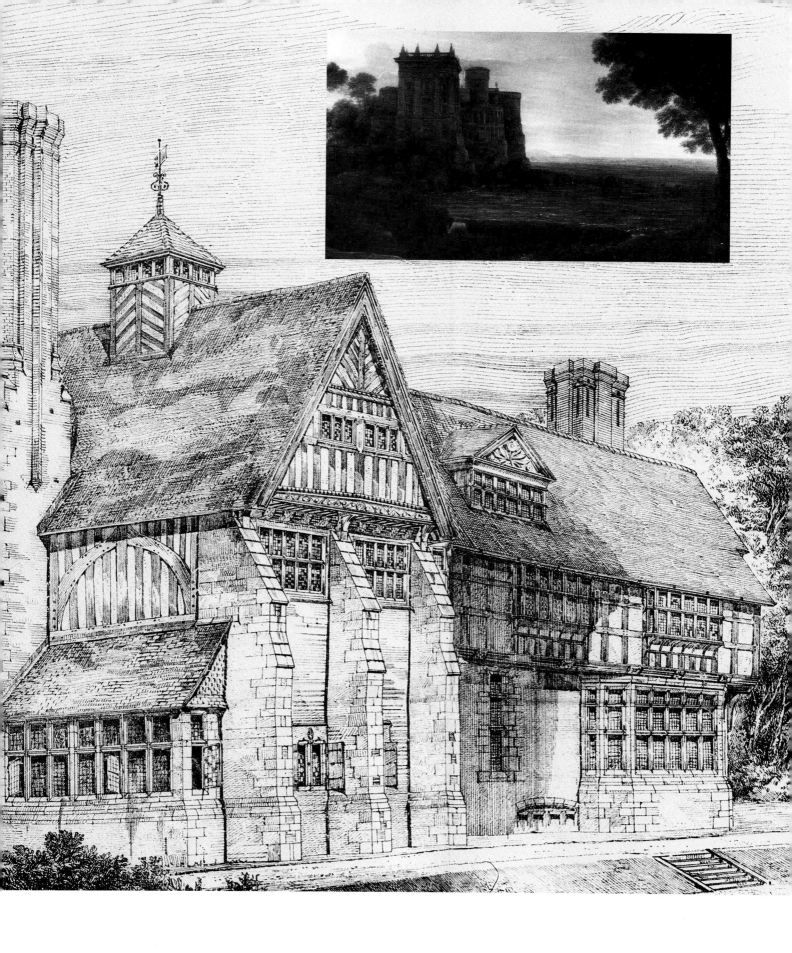

Learning in France

BETWEEN SCHOOL AND UNIVERSITY, *Nicholas is sent to learn French at La Grenadière, a small villa on the Loire kept by M. and Mme Leroy. Here he meets an array of odd characters, including an irascible pair of Scandinavians who play tennis together; he makes progress in French, though not as much as Widmerpool, who is there for the same reason and takes life far more seriously ('This effort to polish up my French is merely in the nature of a holiday . . . I am articled to a firm of solicitors'); and he falls in love with one of the nieces of the family, Suzette.*

Here too he gets a first inkling of Widmerpool's dogged will to succeed. Against all expectations, the latter manages to reconcile the Scandinavians Ørn and Lundquist when they quarrel bitterly over Suzette.

'These things are worth trouble', said Widmerpool. 'You may learn that in time, Jenkins.'

I followed him up the stairs, more than a little impressed. There was something about the obstinacy with which he pursued his aims that could not be disregarded, or merely ridiculed. Even then I did not recognise the quest for power.

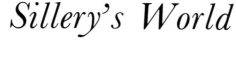

Sillery's World

OF JENKINS'S CAREER AT OXFORD, *what remains most vividly in his (and the reader's) mind are Sillery's afternoon tea-parties,* to which anyone might drop in after half-past three. Action of some law of averages always regulated the numbers at these gatherings to something between four and eight persons, mostly undergraduates, though an occasional don was not unknown. . . . Here a thousand undergraduate attitudes had been penitentially acted out. Youth, dumb with embarrassment, breathless with exhibitionism, stuttering with nerves, inarticulate with conceit. . . . all had obediently leapt through the hoop at Sillery's ringmaster behest.

Professor Sillery, a bachelor don in his fifties, likes young men, but most of all he likes power, the power that comes through hidden contacts and intrigues. His understanding of human nature, coarse, though immensely serviceable, and his unusual ingenuity of mind were both employed ceaselessly in discovering undergraduate connexions which might be of use to him. *The result of these efforts was that* he sometimes found himself able to exercise a respectable modicum of influence in a larger world. That, at least, was how things must have appeared to Sillery himself, and in such activities his spirit was concentrated.

In Sillery's room – 'an untidy room, furnished as he would remark, like a boarding-house parlour' – two men to be important to Nicholas later meet him and each other: J. G. Quiggin and Mark Members, who on this occasion drew away his legs, hitherto stretched the length of the sofa, and brought his knees right up to his chin, clasping his hands round them in the position shown in a picture. . . . called the Boyhood of Raleigh, while he regarded Quiggin with misgiving.

The end of this particular day is to live in Nicholas's memory for reasons of which he has no inkling at the time. When he and Stringham return to the latter's room they find Peter Templer waiting for them with two of his business friends, Bob Duport and Jimmy Brent, ill-mannered and aggressive types for whom Nicholas feels nothing but contempt. The purpose of the visit turns out to be to show off Peter's new (secondhand) Vauxhall. All five set off for a ride in it, pick up two local girls and end up ignominiously in a ditch. Many years later this absurd little incident assumes a special retrospective meaning for Nicholas: of the men in the car, one (Duport) is destined to become the husband of Peter's sister Jean, and another two (himself and Brent) her lovers.

42

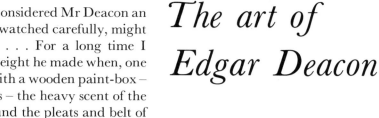

The art of Edgar Deacon

MY PARENTS legitimately considered Mr Deacon an eccentric, who, unless watched carefully, might develop into a bore . . . . For a long time I remembered the impression of height he made when, one day after tea, he presented me with a wooden paint-box – the pigments contained in tubes – the heavy scent of the tobacco he smoked hanging round the pleats and belt of his Norfolk jacket, a garment already beginning to look a little old-fashioned.

Mr Deacon's paintings are also 'beginning to look a little old-fashioned'. Always of classical subjects, they are Pre-Raphaelite in influence without being precisely Pre-Raphaelite in spirit: a compromise between, say, Burne-Jones and Alma-Tadema. (*His 'Boyhood of Cyrus' is later to play a part in Nicholas's life.*) *He disliked the Impressionists, the Post-Impressionists, the Cubists and the Surrealists.* In fact Puvis de Chavannes and Simeon Solomon, the last of whom I think he regarded as his master, were the only painters I ever heard him speak of with unqualified approval.

In the summer of 1919, Nicholas and his parents meet him by chance in the Louvre. When we had come up with him he was inspecting with close attention Perugino's St. Sebastian, for the better examination of which, stooping slightly, he had just produced a small magnifying-glass with a gold rim.

In discussing this picture Mr Deacon shows an unexpected grasp of military hierarchy – at least of a somewhat obsolete order – by pointing out that the Saint, holding as he did the rank of centurion – and being, therefore, a comparatively senior non-commissioned or warrant officer – probably possessed a less youthful and altogether more rugged appearance than that attributed to him by Perugino.

Love in Kensington Gardens

THE LAST *and most serious of Jenkins's early unfulfilled love affairs is with Barbara Goring, the boisterous niece of Lady Walpole-Wilson. Although mildly attracted to her for some time, he does not realize that he is in love with her until one Sunday afternoon in Hyde Park. He meets her by chance with her cousin Eleanor.*

We strolled, all three, towards Kensington Gardens... Eleanor Walpole-Wilson, a square, broad-shouldered girl, rather above the average in height, wore her hair plaited in a bun at the back, which always looked as if it were about to come down at any moment: and did sometimes, in fact, descend piecemeal. She had brought with her Sultan, a labrador, and was trying to train this dog by blasts on a whistle, which she accompanied with harsh, monosyllabic shouting. That enterprise, the training of Sultan, was in keeping with Eleanor's habit of behaviour, as she was always accustomed to act, in principle, as if London were the country: an exercise of will she rarely relaxed.

We ascended the steps of the Albert Memorial and inspected the figures of the Arts and Sciences loitering in high relief round the central mass of that monument. Eleanor, still blowing her whistle fitfully, made some comment regarding the muscles of the bearded male figure belonging to the group called 'Manufactures' which caused Barbara to burst out laughing. This happened on the way down the steps at the south-east corner, approaching the statues symbolising Asia, where, beside the kneeling elephant, the Bedouin forever rests on his haunches in hopeless contemplation of Kensington Gardens' trees and thickets, the blackened sockets of his eyes ranging endlessly over the rich foliage of these oases of the mirage.

For some reason Eleanor's words seemed immensely funny at that moment. Barbara stumbled, and, for a brief second, took my arm. It was then, perhaps, that a force was released no less powerful for its action proving somewhat delayed; for emotions of that kind are not always immediately grasped.... When I said good-bye at the gates I experienced a sense of unaccountable loss.

William Dobell

Dinner in Eaton Square

TAXIS WERE DRAWING UP in the late sunshine before several of the houses in the square, and young men in tails and girls in evening dress, looking rather selfconscious in the bright daylight, were paying fares or ringing front-door bells.

After coming down from university, Jenkins finds a modest job with an art publisher and spends his evenings going to dinners and dances in Mayfair and the West End. One of the most familiar is that of the Walpole-Wilsons in Eaton Square. It is here that he first sees Mr Deacon's painting 'Boyhood of Cyrus'. The canvas, comparatively small for a 'Deacon', evidently not much considered by its owners, had been placed beyond the staircase above a Victorian barometer in a polished mahogany case.

The importance that *Boyhood of Cyrus* eventually assumed had, however, nothing to do with the painter or the merits, such as they were, of the picture itself; its significance being attained simply and solely as a symbol of the probable physical proximity of Barbara Goring, Lady Walpole-Wilson's niece. This association of ideas was, indeed, so powerful that even years after I had ceased to be a guest at the Walpole-Wilson table I could not hear the name 'Cyrus' mentioned – fortunately, in the circumstances, a fairly rare occurrence in everyday life – without being reminded of the pains of early love.

1913: THE KING AND THE CZAR OF RUSSIA
IN A TORCH DANCE IN BERLIN.

The King and Queen visited Berlin in 1913 for the
wedding of Princess Victoria Louise, the Kaiser's
daughter, to Prince Ernest Augustus, on May 24.
Here is seen the bride, with the Czar of Russia and
King George as partners, in a traditional dance.

Table talk

THE GUESTS AT THE WALPOLE-WILSONS' *represent a typical deb dinner party. Sir Gavin* prided himself in combining in his own home tastes of 'the old school' with a progressive point of view in worldly matters. The scented geranium leaf normally to be found floating in the finger-bowls could be attributed to his wife's leaning towards a more exotic way of life.

At the beginning of the dinner, conversation turns upon the statue to be erected to Earl Haig. The subject, as it happened, was one upon which I knew Eleanor to hold decided opinions, and was therefore a question to be avoided, unless driven to conversational extremities, as she much preferred statement to discussion. . . .

'Surely they can find someone who can carve a horse that looks like a horse.' She spoke with truculence even at the outset. (*The horse, as eventually realized by A. F. Hardiman, in 1929, did indeed look like a horse; he was wise enough to follow Lady Haig's suggested model.*)

'I think they ought to have got Mestroviç in the first place,' said Lady Anne, coldly. . . . This unexpected opinion was plainly issued as a challenge. *Mestroviç, a leading Expressionist sculptor from Yugoslavia, would certainly have provided something more dynamic, and Lady Anne was not alone in wanting to see a work like his 'Indian Drawing a Bow' given a setting in London.*

The talk passes to royalty. Sir Gavin remembers the court ball given for the King and Queen when they visited Berlin in 1913.

'For the wedding of the Kaiser's daughter?' Tompsitt added briskly.

'Princess Victoria Louise,' said Sir Gavin, nodding with approval at this scoring of a point by his satellite. 'I went quite by chance, in place of Saltonstall, who – '

'Though, of course, it makes one feel quite ill to think of dancing with a German now,' said Lady Walpole-Wilson, anxiously.

She had taken the war hard.

Another guest is introduced, whom the reader will meet again, Rosie Manasch, 'a lively, gleaming little Jewess in a scarlet frock', and a particular favourite of Sir Gavin's.

She looked quite out of place in this setting; intended by nature to dance veiled, or, perhaps, unveiled, before the throne of some Oriental potentate . . . or occupying herself behind the scenes in all the appetising labyrinth of harem intrigue. There existed the faintest suspicion of blue hairs upon her upper lip, giving her the look of a beauty of the Byronic era.

49

The Huntercombes' dance

AFTER DINNER at the Walpole-Wilsons', the whole party transfers itself to Belgrave Square for a dance given by Lord and Lady Huntercombe. Lady Huntercombe is a society hostess who affects the 'Gainsborough' look, with on one occasion 'a black ribbon round her neck'. She nodded at one in such a way as to indicate enthusiasm, the rather reckless gaiety of a great actress on holiday, one of the moods, comparatively limited in range, to which her hat and general appearance committed her.

The dance is part of the whole elaborate ritual through which eligible young men and girls were expected to meet each other. Everyone used to say that dances bored them; especially those young men . . . who never failed to respond to an invitation, and stayed, night after night, to the bitter end.

The ball took its course; dance-tune following dance-tune and partner following partner. From time to time, throughout the course of the evening, I saw Widmerpool ploughing his way round the room as if rowing a dinghy in rough water, while he talked energetically to girls more often than not unknown to me; though chosen, no doubt, with the care devoted by him to any principle in which he was interested.

Widmerpool is unlucky this evening. Rosie Manasch, whose foot he stumbles over, nicknames him 'the Frog Footman' and the name sticks. Then, at the end of the evening, Barbara Goring accidentally pours a castor of sugar over his head, a traumatic incident, never forgotten. Nicholas comes across him as the guests are leaving. He appeared to have recovered his normal self-possession, such as it was. One of the servants handed him an opera hat, which he opened with a sharp crepitation, placing it on his head at a tilt as we went down the steps together. The night was a little cooler, though still mild enough.

'Which way do you go?' he asked.

'Piccadilly.'

'Are you taxi-ing?'

'I thought I might walk.'

Under the Quadriga

As they walk home *through the empty streets of London after the Huntercombes' ball, Widmerpool is still seething with resentment and (as Nicholas now learns to his surprise) unrequited love for Barbara.*

By this time we had come to Grosvenor Place, in sight of the triumphal arch, across the summit of which, like a vast paper-weight or capital ornament of an Empire clock, the Quadriga's horses, against a sky of indigo and silver, careered desperately towards the abyss. Here our ways divided.

However, they do not part. A chance encounter brings them into contact with Mr Deacon and his little protégée Gypsy Jones, returning from attempts to sell their pacifist broadsheet, 'War Never Pays!' outside Victoria Station.

'We decided to have a cup of coffee at the stall by Hyde Park Corner,' said Mr Deacon, adding with what could only be described as a deep giggle: 'I felt I could venture there chaperoned by Gypsy. Coffee can be very grateful at this hour. Why not join us in a cup?'

We set off up the hill together four abreast: Widmerpool and Gypsy Jones on the flanks. Across the road the coffee stall came into sight, a spot of light round which the scarlet tunics and white equipment of one or two Guardsmen still flickered like the bright wings of moths attracted from nocturnal shadows by a flame. From the park rose the heavy scent of London on a summer night. Here, too, bands could be heard distinctly throbbing. We crossed the road at the island and joined a knot of people round the stall, at the side of which, as if killing time while he waited for a friend late in arrival, an elderly person in a dinner-jacket was very slowly practising the Charleston. . . . Mr Deacon glanced at him with disapproval, but acknowledged, though without warmth, the smirk proffered by a young man in a bright green suit, the uncomfortable colour of which was emphasised by auburn hair, erratically dyed.

Out of the blue the party is joined by Stringham, also in evening dress and on his way to the house of Mrs Andriadis, his current mistress. 'Why not come, all of you? Milly would be delighted . . . Do come. That is, if none of you mind low parties.'

'Mistress of a Royal Personage'

Mrs Andriadis *belongs to a world at once more elevated and socially inferior to that of the Walpole-Wilsons and the Huntercombes, a world of night-clubs, fast living and easy morals. One of their haunts is the Café de Madrid, destined to be burnt into Nicholas's memory one night in 1940 (see p. 110). She is widely believed to have been the* 'mistress of a Royal Personage for a time': a small woman with powder-grey hair, whose faint touch of a Cockney accent, like her coiffure, was evidently retained deliberately as a considered attraction. She was certainly pretty, though the effect was obtained in some indirect and unobtrusive manner. Her dark eyebrows were strongly marked.

Her friends are a Bohemian mixture of the rich, the fashionable, the talented and the outrageous. In one room the carpet had been rolled back, and a hunchback wearing a velvet smoking-jacket was playing an accordion, writhing backwards and forwards as he attached his instrument with demiurgic frenzy . . . . To this music, cheek to cheek, two or three couples were dancing . . . there were people everywhere, and voices sounded through the upper levels of bedroom floors.

Other guests at the same party whom Nicholas now meets for the first time are the dark-haired divorcée, 'Baby' Wentworth, *the girl-friend of Sir Magnus Donners, and* 'Bijou' Ardglass, 'with china-blue eyes and yellow hair' *who later breaks up Bob Duport's marriage with* Jean.

'Shepherd Market.
Quite cheap
but rather noisy'

Nicholas's rooms *are in Shepherd Market, near Piccadilly* – just beside an all-night garage and opposite a block of flats inhabited almost exclusively by tarts. . . . The local prostitutes were rowdy and aggressive . . . [they] quarrelled and shouted all night long: and when business was bad, were not above tapping on the ground-floor windows in the small hours.

Even so, it is for Nicholas an enchanted precinct. Inconvenient, at moments, as a locality: noisy and uncomfortable: stuffy, depressing, unsavoury: yet the ancient houses still retained some vestige of the dignity of another age; while the inhabitants, many of them existing precariously on their bridge earnings or hire of their bodies, were – as more than one novelist had, even in those days, already remarked – not without their seedy glory.

It is to this 'precinct', then, that Nicholas returns after the excitements of his evenings, and in particular after the crowded night when he has attended in succession the Walpole-Wilsons' dinner, the Huntercombes' ball and Mrs Andriadis's party.

It was already quite light in the street, and although the air was fresh, almost breezy, after the atmosphere of the party, there was a hint, even at this early hour, of another sultry day on the way. Narrow streaks of blue were already beginning to appear across the flat surface of a livid sky. The dawn had a kind of heaviness, perhaps of thundery weather in the offing. No one was about, though the hum of an occasional car driving up Park Lane from time to time broke the silence for a few seconds, the sound, mournful as the huntsman's horn echoing in the forest, dying away quickly in the distance. Early morning bears with it a sense of pressure, a kind of threat of what the day will bring forth. I felt unsettled and dissatisfied, though not in the least drunk. On the contrary, my brain seemed to be working all at once with unusual clarity. Indeed, I found myself almost deciding to sit down, as soon as I reached my room, and attempt to compose a series of essays on human life and character in the manner of, say, Montaigne, so icily etched in my mind at that moment appeared the actions and nature of

those with whom that night I had been spending my time. However, second thoughts convinced me that any such efforts at composition would be inadvisable at such an hour. The first thing to do on reaching home would be to try and achieve some sleep. In the morning, literary matters might be reconsidered. I was conscious of having travelled a long way since the Walpole-Wilsons' dinner-party. I was, in fact, very tired.

Shepherd Market is also featured (above) in Michael Arlen's bestseller 'The Green Hat', which Nicholas had read during his first year at university – a novel that I felt painted, on the whole, a sympathetic picture of what London had to offer.

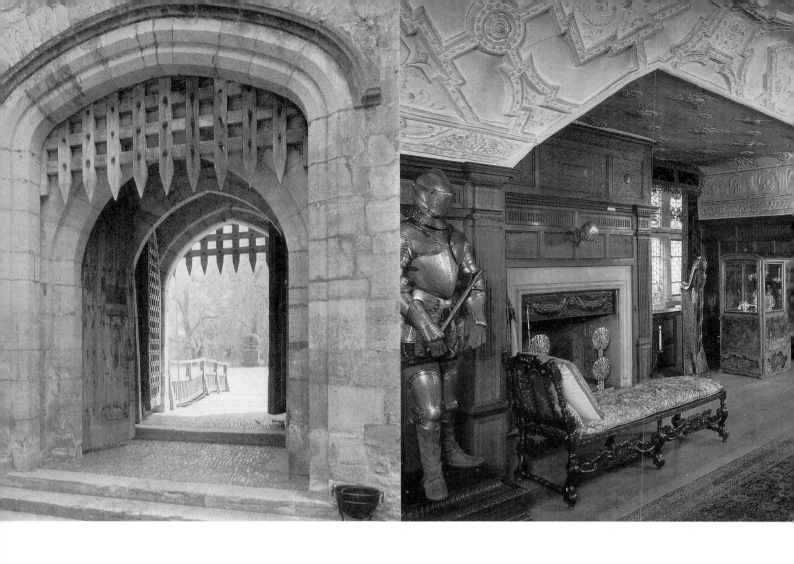

'Where we should put the girls who don't behave'

I
N THE SUMMER OF *1928 or 1929 Nicholas, as one of a large party, is invited to luncheon at Stourwater, the medieval but much restored home of the financier Sir Magnus Donners, at that time the employer of both Stringham and Widmerpool.* The first sight was impressive. Set among oaks and beeches in a green hollow of the land, the castle was approached by a causeway crossing the remains of a moat, a broad expanse of water through which, with great deliberation, a pair of black swans, their passage sending ripples through the pond weed, glided between rushes swaying gently in the warm September air. Here was the Middle Age, from the pages of Tennyson, or Scott, at its most elegant: all sordid and painful elements subtly removed. . . . The cars passed under the portcullis, and across a cobbled quadrangle.

Inside, Nicholas is vaguely disturbed by the heavy furnishings, the works of art, the suits of Gothic armour. But something was decidedly amiss. The final consequence of the pains lavished on these halls and galleries was not precisely that of a Hollywood film set, the objects assembled being, in the first place, too genuine, too valuable; there was even a certain sense of fitness, of historical association more or less correctly assessed. The display was discomforting, not contemptible. . . .

The dining-room was hung with sixteenth-century tapestries. I supposed that they might be Gobelins from their general appearance, and blue and crimson tints, set against lemon yellow. They illustrated the Seven Deadly Sins. I found myself sitting opposite *Luxuria*. . . . In the background, the open doors of a pillared house revealed a

four-poster bed, with hangings rising to an apex, under the canopy of which a couple lay clenched in a priapic grapple. Among trees to the right of the composition, further couples and groups, three or four of them at least, were similarly occupied in smaller houses and Oriental tents; or, in one case, simply on the ground. *The tapestry is clearly in the iconographical tradition represented by Bosch's painted table-top of the Seven Deadly Sins, where Luxuria (Lust) comprises a similar scene.*

Next to Nicholas at table is a girl whom he does not at first recognize: Jean Templer, now married and called Jean Duport. He is again attracted to her and has a curious sudden sense of knowing her all at once much better. . . .

'You were so deep in the tapestry,' she said.

'I was wondering about the couple in the little house on the hill.'

'They have a special devil – or is he a satyr? – to themselves.'

'He seems to be collaborating, doesn't he?'

'Just lending a hand, I think.'

'A guest, I suppose – or a member of the staff?'

'Oh, a friend of the family,' she said. 'All newly-married couples have someone of that sort about. Sometimes several. Didn't you know? I see you can't be married.'

'But how do you know they are newly-married?'

'They've got such a smart little house,' she said. 'They must be newly-married. And rather well off, too, I should say.'

At the end of the evening, Sir Magnus takes his guests on a tour of the house, of which the climax is a visit to the dungeons, something which Sir Magnus particularly enjoys. We came at length to the head of a spiral staircase, leading down to subterranean depths. . . . 'We are now descending to the dungeons,' said Sir Magnus, his voice trembling slightly. 'I sometimes think that is where we should put girls who don't behave.' . . . What perverse refinements, verbal or otherwise, were actually implied by Sir Magnus's words could only be guessed. *Nothing very sinister does in fact happen in the dungeons, but the threat is there; and the subject of Sir Magnus's sexual tastes is one that will continue to fascinate Nicholas almost to the end.*

Mr Deacon's grotto and its naiad

B Y THIS PERIOD OF THE LATE *1920s Mr Deacon has given up painting in favour of a career as antique dealer. His shop is in a shabby street off the Tottenham Court Road in London.* Through the plate glass, obscured in watery depths, dark green like the interior of an aquarium's compartments, Victorian work-tables, *papier-mâché* trays, Staffordshire figures, and a varnished scrap screen – upon the sombrely coloured montage of which could faintly be discerned shiny versions of *Bubbles* and *For He Had Spoken Lightly of a Woman's Name* [*inset*] – swam gently into further aqueous recesses that eddied back into yet more remote alcoves of the double room: additional sub-terranean grottoes, hidden from view, in which, like a grubby naiad, Gypsy Jones, as described so vividly by Mr Deacon, was accustomed, from time to time, to sleep, or at least to recline. . . . For some reason, the thought aroused a faint sense of desire. The exoticism of the place as a bedroom was undeniable.

Gypsy Jones appeals to Nicholas as a sort of gamine version of Barbara Goring. Dedicated to world revolution, aggressive, abrasive ('like a thoroughly ill-conditioned errand boy'), she is nevertheless not unattractive, and when Nicholas calls unexpectedly while she is alone in the shop trying on her costume as Eve for a fancy-dress party, he yields to 'the atmosphere of the alcove' and makes love to her.

This likeness to Barbara was more clearly indicated, however, than by a merely mental comparison of theory, because, while Gypsy lay upon the divan, her hands before her, looking, perhaps rather self-consciously, a little like Goya's *Maja nude* – or possibly it would be nearer the mark to cite that picture's derivation, Manet's *Olympia*, which I had, as it happened, heard her mention on some former occasion – she glanced down, with satisfaction, at her own extremities.

'How brown my leg is,' she said. 'Fancy sunburn lasting that long.' . . . I had been abruptly reminded of Barbara's remark uttered under the trees of Belgrave Square earlier in the year: 'How blue my hand is in the moonlight.' Self-admiration apart, there could be no doubt now that they had a great deal in common.

C. SPENCELAYH.

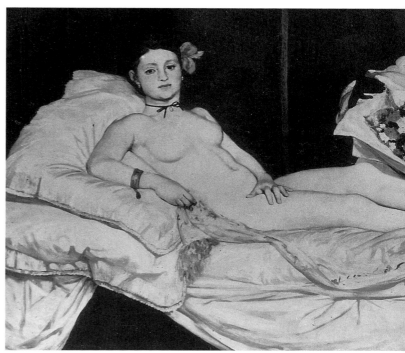

'I don't think you have met Mrs Erdleigh'

SHE WAS BETWEEN FORTY AND FIFTY, perhaps nearer fifty, though possibly her full bosom and style of dress, at a period when it was fashionable to be thin, made her seem a year or two older than her age. Dark red hair piled high on her head in what seemed to me an outmoded style, and good, curiously blurred features from which looked out immense, misty, hazel eyes, made her appearance striking. Her movements, too, were unusual. She seemed to glide rather than walk across the carpet, giving the impression almost of a phantom, a being from another world. . . .

In one sense, Mrs Erdleigh is a being from another world – the world of Dr Trelawney and (later) 'Scorpio' Murtlock. Jenkins first meets her at the Ufford, the seedy Bayswater hotel where his Uncle Giles always stays when in London. It occupied two corner houses in a latent, almost impenetrable region west of the Queen's Road. Not only the battleship-grey colour but also something at once angular and top-heavy about the block's configuration as a whole, suggested a large vessel moored in the street.

Here, one Sunday afternoon in the autumn of 1931 Nicholas is taking tea with Uncle Giles when Mrs Erdleigh unexpectedly joins them. Mrs Erdleigh gazed at me for a second or two before taking my hand, continuing to encircle its fingers even after I had made a slight effort to relax my own grasp. Her palm felt warm and soft, and seemed to exude a mysterious tremor. Scent, vaguely Oriental in its implications, rolled across from her in great stifling waves. The huge liquid eyes seemed to look deep down into my soul, and far, far beyond towards nameless, unexplored vistas of the infinite. . . . I noticed that she wore no wedding ring, carrying in its place on her third finger a large opal, enclosed by a massive gold serpent swallowing its own tail.

Mrs Erdleigh is a mystic, a clairvoyant – and something of a charlatan? But her predictions turn out disconcertingly often to be correct. Inevitably, conversation at the Ufford turns to astrology, to birth-signs, to the future. A pack of cards is produced, 'grey and greasy with use.' First she reads Uncle Giles's future. There was a good deal of opposition to his 'plans', perhaps not surprisingly; also, it was true, much gossip, even some calumny surrounded him. 'Don't forget you have Saturn in the Twelfth House', Mrs Erdleigh remarked in an aside. 'Secret enemies.'

She goes on to Nicholas himself – 'I expect *he* wants to hear about *love.*' *She foresees a woman in his life.* 'I think you have run across her once or twice before, though not recently. But there seems to be another man interested, too. He might even be a husband. You don't like him much. He is tallish, I should guess. Fair, possibly red hair. In business. Often goes abroad.'

It is a speech that Nicholas will remember when he meets Jean again.

Cupid 34

A dark-haired woman 49

The parlour sibyl

La Sibylle des Salons.

Enemy 8

Gossip 20

'New positions in the dance'

ONE EVENING *in 1932 Nicholas is sitting in the palm court of the Ritz Hotel, waiting for someome in connection with his publishing work. A party of South Americans is gathered underneath the bronze nymph at the end of the room.* Away on her pinnacle, the nymph seemed at once a member of this Latin family party, and yet at the same time morally separate from them: an English girl, perhaps, staying with relations possessing business interests in South America, herself in love for the first time after a visit to some neighbouring estancia. Now she had strayed away from her hosts to enjoy delicious private thoughts in peace while she examined the grimacing face of the river-god carved in stone on the short surface of wall by the grotto. Pensive, quite unaware of the young tritons violently attempting to waft her away from the fountain by sounding their conches at full blast, she gazed full of wonder that no crystal stream gushed from the water-god's contorted jaws. Perhaps in such a place she expected a torrent of champagne. Although stark naked, the nymph looked immensely respectable; less provocative, indeed, than some of the fully dressed young women seated below her, whose olive skins and silk stockings helped to complete this most unwintry scene.

The publishing contact fails to arrive, but instead Nicholas runs into Peter Templer, his new wife Mona and (for the third time) Peter's sister Jean, now married and separated from Bob Duport. They all have dinner together at the Ritz Grill, a dinner which seemed to partake of the nature of a ritual feast, a rite from which the four of us emerged to take up new positions in the formal dance with which human life is concerned.

At the end of the dinner Peter invites Nicholas back to their house at Maidenhead for the weekend.

'You must come,' said Jean, speaking in her matter-of-fact tone, almost as if she were giving an order. 'There are all sorts of things I want to talk about'. . . .

While we were at dinner heavy snow was descending outside. . . . A few flakes were still blowing about in the clear winter air when we set out at last for the Templers' house. The wind had suddenly dropped. The night was very cold. . . .

Mona, now comatose after the wine at dinner, rolled herself up in a rug and took the seat in front. Almost immediately she went to sleep. Jean and I sat at the back of the car. We passed through Hammersmith, and the neighbourhood of Chiswick: then out on to the Great West Road. For a time I made desultory conversation. At last she scarcely answered, and I gave it up. Templer, smoking a cigar in the front, also seemed disinclined to talk now that he was at the wheel. We drove along at a good rate. . . .

The exact spot must have been a few hundred yards beyond the point where the electrically illuminated young lady in a bathing dress dives eternally through the petrol-tainted air; night and day, winter and summer, never reaching the water of the pool to which she endlessly glides. Like some image of arrested development, she returns for ever, voluntarily, to the springboard from which she started her leap. A few seconds after I had seen this bathing belle journeying, as usual, imperturbably through the frozen air, I took Jean in my arms.

Her response, so sudden and passionate, seemed surprising only a minute or two later. All at once everything was changed. Her body felt at the same time hard and yielding, giving a kind of glow as if live current issued from it. I used to wonder afterwards whether, in the last resort, of all the time we spent together, however ecstatic, those first moments on the Great West Road were not the best.

Cinema interludes

IT WAS A PERIOD OF MY LIFE [1933], when in recollection I seem often to have been standing in a cinema queue with a different girl.

The impression is that Nicholas sees innumerable films, but in fact he mentions only two titles, both of them films with serious artistic pretensions – Leontine Sagan's 'Mädchen in Uniform', and Robert Flaherty's 'Man of Aran'. Both turn out to be connected in his life with Mona, the beautiful model whom Peter Templer has married. When Nicholas encounters Templer in the Ritz, he is waiting for his wife, and when she arrives he realizes that they had met at a party of Mr Deacon's. I asked when she was due at the Ritz.

'When she comes out of the cinema,' he said. 'She was determined to see *Mädchen in Uniform*. I couldn't face it. After all, one meets quite enough lesbians in real life without going to the pictures to see them.'

'But it isn't a film about lesbians.'

'Oh, isn't it?' said Templer. 'Mona thought it was. She'll be disappointed if you're right.'

About a year later, we find Nicholas queuing (with girl) for 'Man of Aran'. During the eternity of time that always precedes the termination of the 'big picture', I had even begun to wonder whether we should spend the rest of our days on that particular stretch of London pavement, when, at long last, just as rain had begun to fall, the portals of the auditorium burst open to void the patrons of the earlier performance. First came those scattered single figures, who as if distraught by what they have seen and seeking to escape at whatever the cost, hurry blindly from the building, they care not how, nor where; then the long serpentine of spectators to whom expulsion into the street means no more than the need to take another decision in life.

Among those emerging is J. G. Quiggin, Jenkins's contemporary at university, now making a name for himself as a critic, and the man for whom Mona has left Peter Templer. Quiggin throws out a hasty invitation for Nicholas to visit him and Mona in the country. Then the queue moves forward and they are parted. We passed into the darkness and *Man of Aran*.

Films are more than an amusement for Nicholas. He is working as a script writer in a film studio with Chips Lovell, who eventually becomes his brother-in-law. 'To be a script writer was at that period the ambition of almost everyone who could hold a pen.' The films that he and Chips actually write are never specified, and, one feels, are being deliberately hushed-up by Nicholas. But a job such as adapting A. E. W. Mason's novel 'Drums' for the screen is typically one that might have required his talents.

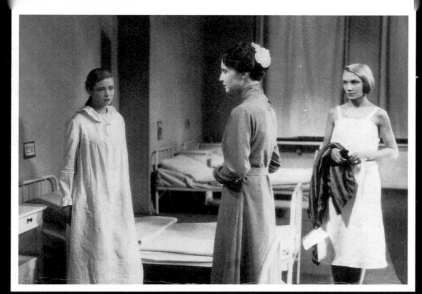
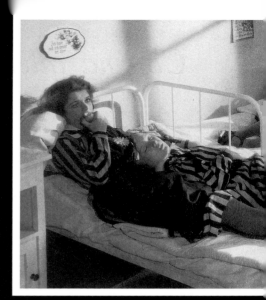

The faces of Jean

NICHOLAS'S RELATIONSHIP WITH JEAN, *begun at Peter Templer's house in Maidenhead, develops into the major love affair of his life before his marriage. When he met her again at the Ritz, he had already been conscious of a deepening interest, which becomes more and more intense.*

She was taller than I remembered, and carried herself well. Her face, like her brother's, had become a shade fuller, a change that had coarsened his appearance, while in her the sharp, almost animal look I remembered was now softened. She had not entirely lost her air of being a school-girl; though certainly, it had to be admitted, a very smartly dressed school-girl. I thought to myself, not without complacence, that I was able to appreciate her without in any way losing my head, as I might once have done. There was still a curious fascination about her grey-blue eyes, slanting a little, as it were caught tightly between soft, lazy lids and dark, luxurious lashes. Once she had reminded me of Rubens's *Chapeau de Paille*. Now for some reason – though there was not much physical likeness between them – I thought of the woman smoking the hookah in Delacroix's *Femmes d'Alger dans leur appartement*. Perhaps there was something of the odalisque about Jean, too.

Separated from her husband, Bob Duport, she lives in a flat somewhere beyond Rutland Gate, another district of London that becomes soaked in associations for Nicholas.

I rang the bell of the ground-floor flat. . . . For some time there was no answer to the ring. I waited, peering through the frosted glass of the front door, feeling every second an eternity. Then the door opened a few inches and Jean looked out. I saw her face only for a moment. She was laughing.

'Come in,' she said quickly. 'It's cold.'

As I entered the hall, closing the door behind me, she ran back along the passage. I saw that she wore nothing but a pair of slippers.

'There is a fire in here,' she called from the sitting-room.

I hung my hat on the grotesque piece of furniture, designed for that use, that stood by the door. Then I followed her down the passage and into the room. The furniture and decoration of the flat were of an appalling banality.

'Why are you wearing no clothes?'
'Are you shocked?'
'What do you think?'
'I think you are.'
'Surprised, rather than shocked.'
'To make up for the formality of our last meeting.'
'Aren't I showing my appreciation?'
'Yes, but you must not be so conventional.'
'But if it had been the postman?'
'I could have seen through the glass.'
'He, too, perhaps.'
'I had a dressing-gown handy.'
'It was a kind thought, anyway.'
'You like it?'
'Very much.'
'Tell me something nice.'
'This style suits you.'
'Not too *outré*?'
'On the contrary.'
'Is this how you like me?'
'Just like this.'
There is, after all, no pleasure like that given by a woman who really wants to see you.

General Conyers: 'Abreast of the times'

Wᴇ ʜᴀᴅ ᴋɴᴏᴡɴ Gᴇɴᴇʀᴀʟ Cᴏɴʏᴇʀs immemorially not because my father had ever served under him but through some long-forgotten connexion with my mother's parents. *In 1914, when we first meet him, he has retired from active service and is a member of the Royal Body Guard, a ceremonial post which he took up after his marriage at the age of nearly fifty.*

Conyers has had a distinguished military career, winning especial renown in the Boer War. This incident is described, none too precisely, by Uncle Giles: 'After French moved over the Modder River, the whole Cavalry Division was ordered to charge. . . . [Conyers] got himself into the charge somehow. Hadn't any business with the cavalry brigades. Put up some excuse. Then, a day or two later, went back to where he ought to have been in the first place. Made himself most officious among the transport wagons. Line of march was like Hyde Park at the height of the Season, so a fellow who was in the advance told me – carriages end to end in Albert Gate – and Conyers running about cursing and swearing as if he owned the place.'

For a man of his background, Conyers has an unexpectedly wide range of interests, and Nicholas is constantly being surprised by some new facet of his personality. Although no great performer he had always loved playing the 'cello, and on retirement occupied much of his time with music. *Taking tea with the Conyers in the thirties, Nicholas notes:* a low melancholy wailing began all at once to echo from somewhere not far off, persistent, though muffled by several doors: notes of a hidden orchestra, mysterious, even a shade unearthly, as if somewhere in the vicinity gnomes were thumbing strange instruments in a cave. . . .

'Aylmer will be with us in a minute,' said Mrs Conyers. 'He always practises until five o'clock when we are in London.'

The conversation turns first to literature (the general has been reading Virginia Woolf's 'Orlando') and then: 'Now, psychoanalysis. Ever read anything about that? . . . Been reading a lot about it recently. . . . Freud – Jung – haven't much use for Adler. Something in it, you know. Tells you why you do things.'

Later, when Widmerpool's engagement to Mrs Haycock (Mrs Conyers' sister) is broken off, he is ready with a cogent psychological explanation.

'It seems to me,' said the General, 'that he is a typical intuitive extravert – classical case, almost. Cold-blooded, keen on a thing for a moment, but never satisfied. Wants to get on to something else. . . . You're going to say you are a hard-bitten Freudian, and won't hear of Jung and his ideas. Very well, I'll open another field of fire.'

(This 'mandala' was produced by a female patient of Jung, illustrating some of the archetypes in the collective unconscious.)

At Lady Molly's

LADY MOLLY *enters Jenkins's life through his colleague at the film studio, Chips Lovell, whose aunt she is. (Later she comes to be connected to Nicholas by marriage.) Her first husband had been the Marquess of Sleaford; her second is Ted Jeavons, 'not a bad chap at all,' according to Chips, 'though of a rather unglamorous background.' The Jeavons house, in the Gloucester Road area of London, is a meeting place for a varied collection of people from different walks of life.*

Lovell stopped in front of a fairly large house of dark red brick, the architecture of which sounded a distant, and not particularly encouraging, echo of the High Renaissance. . . .

I followed him to the first floor; and into a double drawing-room in which eight or nine persons were standing or sitting. A general though never precisely defined suggestion of chinoiserie, sustained by a profusion of Oriental bowls and jars, pervaded the decoration. Some of the furniture was obviously rather valuable; the rest, gimcrack to a degree. Pictures showed a similar variation of standard, a Richard Wilson and a Greuze (these I noted later) hanging among pastels of Moroccan native types.

Mona: 'A beautiful girl by any standards'

MONA BEGAN HER CAREER *as a black-haired model in the circle of Gypsy Jones. From there she graduated to more profitable work in advertising, becoming a blonde in the process. Nicholas meets her again at the Ritz, when she has been married to Peter Templer for a year (see p. 64) and is immediately aware that he has seen her before.* Then I remembered that he had warned me I should recognise the stylised, conventionally smiling countenance, set in blonde curls, that formerly appeared so often, on the walls of buses and underground trains, advocating a well-known brand of toothpaste. She must have been nearly six foot in height: in spite of a rather coarse complexion, a beautiful girl by any standards.

Married to Peter Templer, Mona assumes the role expected of her of a society beauty, rich, spoiled, and bored. With the extraordinary adaptability of women, she had managed to alter considerably the lines of her figure, formerly a striking synthesis of projections and concavities that certainly seemed to demand immediate expression in bronze or stone. Now her body had been disciplined into a fashionable, comparatively commonplace mould. *But*

her marriage to Peter Templer is already wearing thin. At the weekend party that follows the evening at the Ritz Mona's sulkiness cast a gloom over the house. . . . She was like some savage creature, anxious to keep up appearances before members of a more highly civilized species, though at the same time keenly aware of her own superiority in cunning. There was something hard and untamed about her, probably the force that had attracted Templer and others.

Her interest turns from Templer to Quiggin, less polished but more direct and morally committed. In going to live with him she gives up the luxury she had previously enjoyed. Nicholas has the chance to observe them at close quarters when they are staying in a cottage on the Thrubworth estate. She looked far less trim than when married to Templer . . . wearing . . . an outfit not much suited to the country, she retained a kind of shabby smartness of appearance.

We get a glimpse of Mona through Jean's eyes when she sends Nicholas a French postcard showing a man and a woman sitting literally one on top of the other in an armchair upholstered with crimson plush. These two exchanged ardent glances. They were evidently on the best of terms, because the young man, fair, though at the same time rather semitic of feature, was squeezing the girl's arm just above the elbow. . . .

'Doesn't she look like Mona?' Jean had written on the back.

Hugh Moreland

JENKINS FIRST MEETS *the composer Hugh Moreland about 1928 and they become close friends. Characteristically, Jenkins offers no opinions of his own on Moreland's music, but we are left in no doubt that he is a genius. It is known that his original in real life was Constant Lambert, though the parallel is by no means exact, or even outwardly very close. Lambert destroyed his own brilliant career at the age of 46. Moreland too dies young (about 55), but his life is more sober and conventional. Like Lambert, he is a trenchant critic and theorist, a personality of wit and charm. Christopher Wood's portrait of Lambert (left) shows him in his twenties, at about the time when Nicholas would have met Moreland. Nicholas compares him to the young Beethoven and also to the figure of Folly in Bronzino's 'Allegory of Time' (another intrusion of Time as a real presence into the fabric of the story).*

He was formed physically in a 'musical' mould, classical in type, with a massive, Beethoven-shaped head, high forehead, temples swelling outwards, eyes and nose somehow bunched together in a way to make him glare at times like a High Court Judge about to pass sentence. On the other hand, his short, dark, curly hair recalled a dissipated cherub, a less aggressive, more intellectual version of Folly in Bronzino's picture, rubicund and mischievous, as he threatens with a fusillade of rose petals the embrace of Venus and Cupid; while Time in the background, whiskered like the Emperor Franz-Josef, looms behind a blue curtain as if evasively vacating the bathroom. Moreland's face in repose, in spite of this cherubic, humorous character, was not without melancholy too; his flush suggesting none of that riotously healthy physique enjoyed by Bronzino's – and, I suppose, everyone else's – Folly.

Moves to the left

DURING THE DEPRESSION *many of the characters in Jenkins's intellectual world shift significantly to the left. Quiggin is already there; Mona, having left Peter for him, adopts the same position. Even the established romantic novelist St John Clarke is converted by Quiggin to Communism and takes part in a Hunger Marchers' Demonstration in Hyde Park, at which Sillery is also present.* I allowed my attention to be distracted for a moment by Sillery's voice shouting in high, almost jocular tones: 'Abolish the Means Test!'

But the only true revolutionary in Jenkins's story is Gypsy Jones, 'La Pasionaria of Hendon Central', as Moreland calls her. In the summer of 1939 Nicholas catches a glimpse of Gypsy in action addressing a street meeting.

Two women in trousers were hawking a newspaper or pamphlet. . . . Our attention was engaged by a new speaker. This was the second newspaper-selling woman, who, having now handed over her papers to the man with the cloth cap, herself jumped on to the soapbox. In a harsh clear voice she opened a tremendous tirade, quite different in approach from the quieter, more reasoned appeal of the spectacled man.

'. . . blooming bloody hypocrisy . . . . anybody wants this war except a few crackpots . . . see a chance of seizing world power and grinding the last miserable halfpence from the frozen fingers of stricken mankind . . . lot of Fascist, terroristic, anti-semitic, war-mongering, exploiting White Guards and traitors to the masses. . .'

It was Gypsy Jones. I had not set eyes on her since the days when we used to meet in Mr Deacon's antique shop. She had lost a front tooth, otherwise did not look greatly changed from what she had been in the Mr Deacon period: older, harder, angrier, further than ever from her last bath, but essentially the same. Her hair was still cut short like a boy's, her fists clenched, her legs set wide apart. Over her trousers she wore a man's overcoat, far from new, the aggressive inelegance of the ensemble expressing to perfection her own revolutionary, destructive state of mind. . . . '. . . not appealing to a lot of half-baked Bloomsbury intellectuals and Hampstead ideologues . . . bourgeois scabs and parlour-socialist nancy boys . . . scum of weak-kneed Trotskyite flunkeys . . . betraying the workers and anyone else it suits their filthy bloody blackleg book to betray . . . I'm talking about politics – socialism – reality – adaptability . . .'

After the war, in 1946, she strikes Nicholas as short, wiry, her hair tied up in a red handkerchief, somehow calling to mind old-fashioned Soviet posters celebrating the Five Year Plan. *But she is now married to the publisher and former proprietor of the Vox Populi Press, (lately created Sir Howard Craggs for his wartime services) and her revolutionary ardour has subsided into a tough but more limited hard-headedness.*

Thrubworth Park

THRUBWORTH *is the seat of the Tolland family, and the home of its head, Lord Warminster, known as Erridge.* A seventeenth-century mansion . . . brick at the back and fronted in the eighteenth century with stone. The façade faced away from us across a wide stretch of lawn. *In the winter of 1934, when Nicholas is staying with Quiggin and Mona, they are invited to dinner there. Erridge has closed most of the house, the state rooms lying abandoned, and the furniture covered in dust-sheets.*

He pulled away the dust-sheets without ceremony; leaving in the centre of the room a heap of linen on the floor. The furniture was on the whole mediocre; although, as at the Jeavonses', there was a good piece here and there. The pictures, too, apart from the Lawrence – the bravura of which gave it some charm – were wholly lacking in distinction. Erridge seemed aware of these deficiencies, referring more than once to the 'rubbish' his forebears had accumulated. Yet, at the same time, in his own peculiar way, he seemed to enjoy this opportunity of displaying the house, a guilty enjoyment, though for that reason no less keen.

Erridge's guilt stems from the fact that he holds left-wing views, and has never been able to reconcile this radical stance with his position as a landed aristocrat. His own rooms are in the old servants' quarters and are as unopulent as possible. A dark wallpaper and heavy mahogany furniture, not very different in style to that exiled to the back parts of the house through which we had passed, made the room seem smaller than its real extent, which was considerable. There were no pictures, though rectangular discoloured patches on the walls showed where frames had once hung. Over the fireplace a chart which I took to be the Tolland pedigree, but on closer examination proved to illustrate in descending scale some principle of economic distribution. Shelves holding more books – classics, Baedekers and a couple of bound copies of the *Boy's Own Paper* – covered the far wall. (It was, *Nicholas tells himself years later,* Erry's only vice, though one he tried to keep dark, as showing in himself a lack of earnestness and sense of social obligation.) At the end of the room stood a table littered with current newspapers and magazines. Another smaller table had been laid with four places, for a meal.

It was clear that Erridge lived and moved and had his being in this room. I wondered whether he also spent his nights there on the sofa. Such rough and ready accommodation might easily be in keeping with his tenets: except that the sofa looked rather too comfortable to assuage at night-time his guilt for being rich. *These 'tenets' will eventually take Erridge to the Republican side in the Spanish Civil War. But before that he goes on a long-meditated trip to China, taking with him, to everyone's surprise, Mona Templer, who is already tiring of Quiggin.*

Westminster and Pimlico

THE VARIOUS DISTRICTS OF LONDON *are strongly differentiated in Nicholas's mind, partly through their local character but even more through their association with people and episodes in his own life.*

The area round Westminster Cathedral has a distinct aura of Widmerpool. Here for many years he has shared a flat with his mother, and here Nicholas visits them around 1928. They lived, as Widmerpool had described, on the top floor of one of the smaller erections of flats in the neighbourhood of Westminster Cathedral. . . . For some reason, perhaps the height of the tower, or more probably the prodigal inappropriateness to London of the whole structure's architectural style, the area immediately adjacent to the cathedral imparts a sense of vertigo, a dizziness almost alarming in its intensity: lines and curves of red brick appearing to meet in a kind of vortex, rather than to be ranged in normal forms of perspective. . . . The lift, like an ominously creaking funicular, swung me up to these mountainous regions, and to a landing where light shone through frosted panes of glass. *Mrs Widmerpool is around fifty, but* her well-preserved appearance was in striking contrast to Widmerpool's own somewhat decaying youth, so that the pair of them appeared almost more like contemporaries, even husband and wife, rather than mother and son. *Widmerpool himself reminds Nicholas of Samuel Pepys.* He had the same obdurate, put-upon, bad-tempered expression. Only a full-bottomed wig was required to complete the picture. True, Widmerpool showed none of Pepys's sensibility where the arts were concerned; in the aesthetic field he was a void. But they had a common preoccupation with money and professional advancement; also a kind of dogged honesty.

Pimlico is the home of the music critic Maclintick, a dedicated, scholarly and perceptive admirer of Moreland, whose life is blighted by his marriage to the termagant Audrey, and who ends as a suicide. We took a bus to Victoria, then passed on foot into a vast desolate region of stucco streets and squares upon which a doom seemed to have fallen. The gloom was cosmic. We traversed these pavements for some distance, proceeding from haunts of seedy, grudging gentility into an area of indeterminate, but on the whole increasingly unsavoury, complexion.

'Maclintick is devoted to this part of London,' Moreland said. 'I am not sure that I agree with him. He says his mood is for ever Pimlico. . . .'

The house, when we reached it, turned out to be a small, infinitely decayed two-storey dwelling that had seen better days; now threatened by a row of mean shops advancing from one end of the street and a fearful slum crowding up from the other.

Maclintick himself is described as 'calculatedly humdrum'. The minute circular lenses of his gold-rimmed spectacles, set across the nose of a pug dog, made me think of caricatures of Thackeray or President Thiers, imposing upon him the air of a bad-tempered doctor.

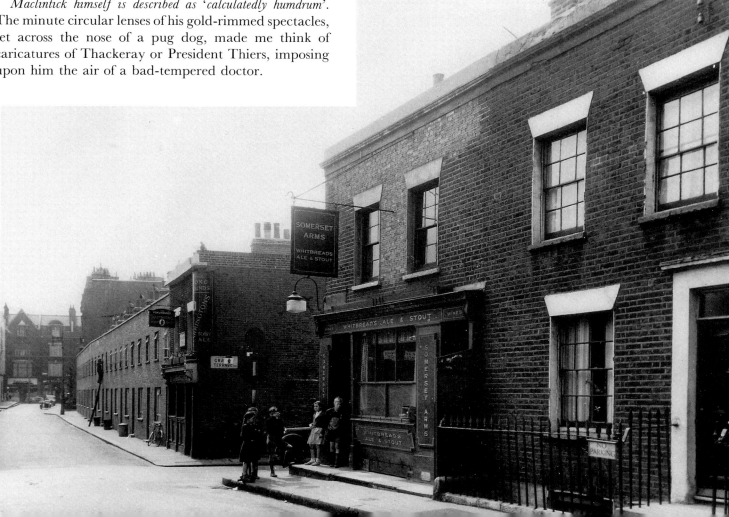

Barnby's world

NICHOLAS'S ACQUAINTANCE *with the artist Ralph Barnby went back to about 1928, when he called at Mr Deacon's shop and found Barnby, the lodger, the only one at home. Through him he enters the Bohemian world of artists, musicians and writers whose rendezvous are the pubs and cafés of Soho and Bloomsbury.*

Only since knowing Barnby had I begun to frequent such society as was collected that night at the Mortimer, which, although it soon enough absorbed me, still at that time represented a world of high adventure. The hiatus between coming down from university and finding some place for myself in London had comprised, with some high spots, an eternity of boredom.

The Mortimer is the Soho pub where Barnby, the composer Moreland and their friends choose to congregate. Even in these days it was regarded by the enlightened as a haunt of 'bores'; but, although the beer was indifferent and the saloon bar draughty, a sprinkling of those connected with the arts, especially musicians, was usually to be found there. . . . Barnby had not yet arrived when I came into the bar, which was emptier than usual. Two or three elderly women dressed in black, probably landladies off duty, were drinking Guinness and grumbling in one corner.

Equally prominent in the lives of all of them are the cafés and restaurants, each with its particular character, ambience and clientèle – Casanova's Chinese Restaurant (based, without much disguise, on Maxim's, a resort of prostitutes in the twenties), the Strasbourg, Foppa's (an upstairs club over a café), the genteel Trouville, patronized by Uncle Giles, or the Hay Loft in Tottenham Court Road, where bacon and eggs could be procured at any hour of the day or night.

Round the corner from the last-named stood Mr Deacon's shop (see p. 60), 'between a French polisher's and the Vox Populi Press,' *the left-wing publishing house run by Howard Craggs, employer and lover of Gypsy Jones.*

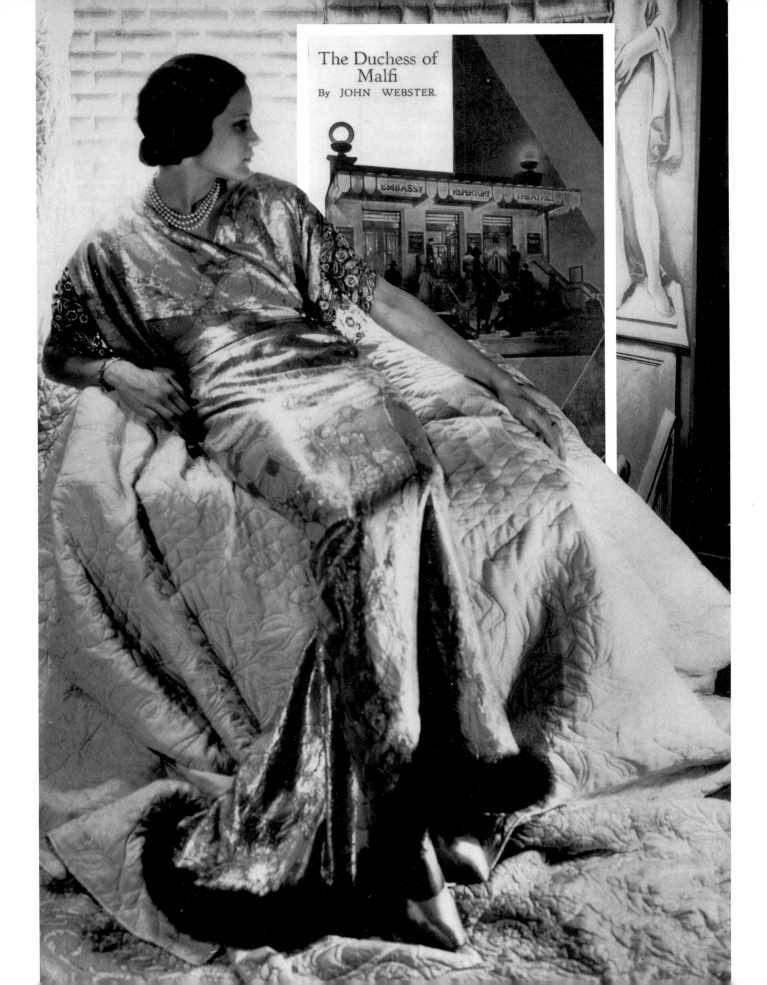

The Duchess of
Malfi
By JOHN WEBSTER.

EMBASSY REPERTORY THEATRE

Matilda

WE MEET MATILDA at the theatre, where she has a part in 'The Duchess of Malfi', and a certain air of theatricality never quite leaves her – not least in the way episodes from her past keep emerging with dramatic effect. Moreland is in love with her. Nicholas goes with him to see her performance at a small theatre situated somewhere off the beaten track.

When at last Matilda Wilson appeared as Julia, Moreland's face took on a look of intensity, almost of strain, more like worry than love. I had been looking forward to seeing her with the interest one feels in being shown for the first time the woman a close friend proposes to marry; for I now had no doubt from the manner in which the evening had been planned that Matilda must be the girl whom Moreland had in mind when he had spoken of taking a wife. . . .

When the play was over, we went round to the stage door, penetrating into regions where the habitually cramped accommodation of theatrical dressing-rooms was more than usually in evidence. . . . We found Matilda Wilson's room at last. She was wearing hardly any clothes, removing her make-up, while Norman Chandler, dressed in a mauve dressing-gown of simulated brocade, sat on a stool beside her, reading a book.

Norman Chandler is another theatrical personality – actor, ballet-dancer and (in Nicholas's words) 'chorus boy'. Socially, his great achievement is to captivate Mrs Foxe, Stringham's mother, with whom he develops an intimate though sexually ambiguous relationship.

'Norman obviously represents the physical type of the future,' Moreland said. . . . The great artists have always decided beforehand what form looks are to take in the world, and Norman is pure Picasso – one of those attenuated, androgynous mountebanks of the Blue Period, who haven't had a meal for weeks.'

'Come along, sweetie, and don't talk so much,' said Matilda, closing her bag and getting up from the dressing-table. 'If we don't have something to eat pretty soon we shall become attenuated, androgynous mountebanks ourselves.'

Moreland succeeds in marrying Matilda. The marriage does not last, although, years later, I had the impression Moreland had never managed to fall entirely out of love with her. *She goes back to a former lover, Sir Magnus Donners, and marries him, taking her place with ease in high society.*

Matilda, looking decidedly smart in a dress of blue and black stripes, was standing beside her husband, talking to the Portuguese ambassador. . . . To be rather older suited her; that or being married to a member of the Cabinet. She had dyed her hair a reddish tint that suited her, too, set off the large green eyes, which were always her most striking feature.

'The Beau Brummell of the new reign'

WIDMERPOOL *has been steadily rising in the City, attaining an expertise in financial matters that wins him respect and – more significantly – power. His ambition is stirred by King Edward's affair with Mrs Simpson, which seems to promise an undreamt-of opening for his particular behind-the-scenes talents.*

'I have been moving in rather exalted circles lately,' he said, giving a very satisfied smile.

'Indeed?'

'Not exactly royal – that is hardly the word yet. . . . You understand me . . . ?'

'I think so.'

'It was an interesting experience.'

'Have you actually met . . .'

Widmerpool bowed his head, suggesting by this movement the knowledge of enviable secrets. At the same time he would allow no admission that might be thought compromising either to himself or those in high places whose reputation must rightly be shielded. I tried to extort more from him without any success.

'When did this happen?'

'Please do not press me for details.'

Quiggin's view of the matter is predictably more direct: If the country must have a king, I consider it desirable, indeed essential that he should marry a divorcée. Two divorces – double as good. I am no friend of the civilisation of Big Business, but at least an American marriage is better than affiliation with our own so-called aristocracy.

In the end, the whole subject subsides with hardly a trace. As it turned out, once the step had been taken, the Abdication became a matter of history, everything resumed an accustomed routine with much greater ease than popularly foreseen. *For everyone, that is, except Widmerpool.*

'I never saw a man so put out by the Abdication,' said Lovell. 'It might have been Widmerpool himself who'd had to abdicate. My goodness, he had taken it to heart.'

'What specially upset him?'

'So far as I could gather, he had cast himself for a brilliant social career if things had worked out differently.'

'The Beau Brummell of the new reign?'

'Not far short of that.'

89

Diverse opinions

THE ETERNAL ONLOOKER *Nicholas Jenkins tells us nothing about his own political beliefs. Events on the national and international stage are important only insofar as they affect people's private lives, and those with strong political (or indeed religious) convictions – from Gypsy Jones to Widmerpool – are presented with a sort of bemused objectivity.*

In 1936 the great topic preoccupying the country was the Spanish Civil War. One Sunday Nicholas lunches with Lady Warminster, his wife Isobel's stepmother. Quiggin is already actively involved: 'Medical supplies for Spanish Loyalists,' said Quiggin, pronouncing the words with quiet doggedness. 'Basque children – there is plenty to do for those with a political conscience.'

More unexpected is the news that Erridge plans to go to Spain to join the International Brigade.

'I don't know whether he will actually fight,' *says his brother Robert.* 'As you know, he holds pacifist views. However, he will certainly be on the opposite side to General Franco. We can at least be sure of that. I can't think that Erry will be any great help to any army he joined, can you?' . . .

'I hope he will try to persuade his friends not to burn *all* the churches', said Lord Huntercombe.

Erridge's exploits in Spain remain more or less speculation among his family and he returns broken in health in 1937. Quiggin dismisses his efforts with scorn:

'Alf seems to have shown a good deal of political obtuseness – perhaps I should say childlike innocence. He appears to have treated POUM, FAI, CNT, and UGT as if they were all the same left-wing extension of the Labour Party. I was not surprised to hear that he was going to be arrested at the time he decided to leave Spain. If you can't tell the difference between a Trotskyite Communist, an Anarcho-Syndicalist, and a properly paid-up Party Member, you had better keep away from the barricades.'

'You had indeed.'

'It is not fair to the workers.'

'Certainly not.'

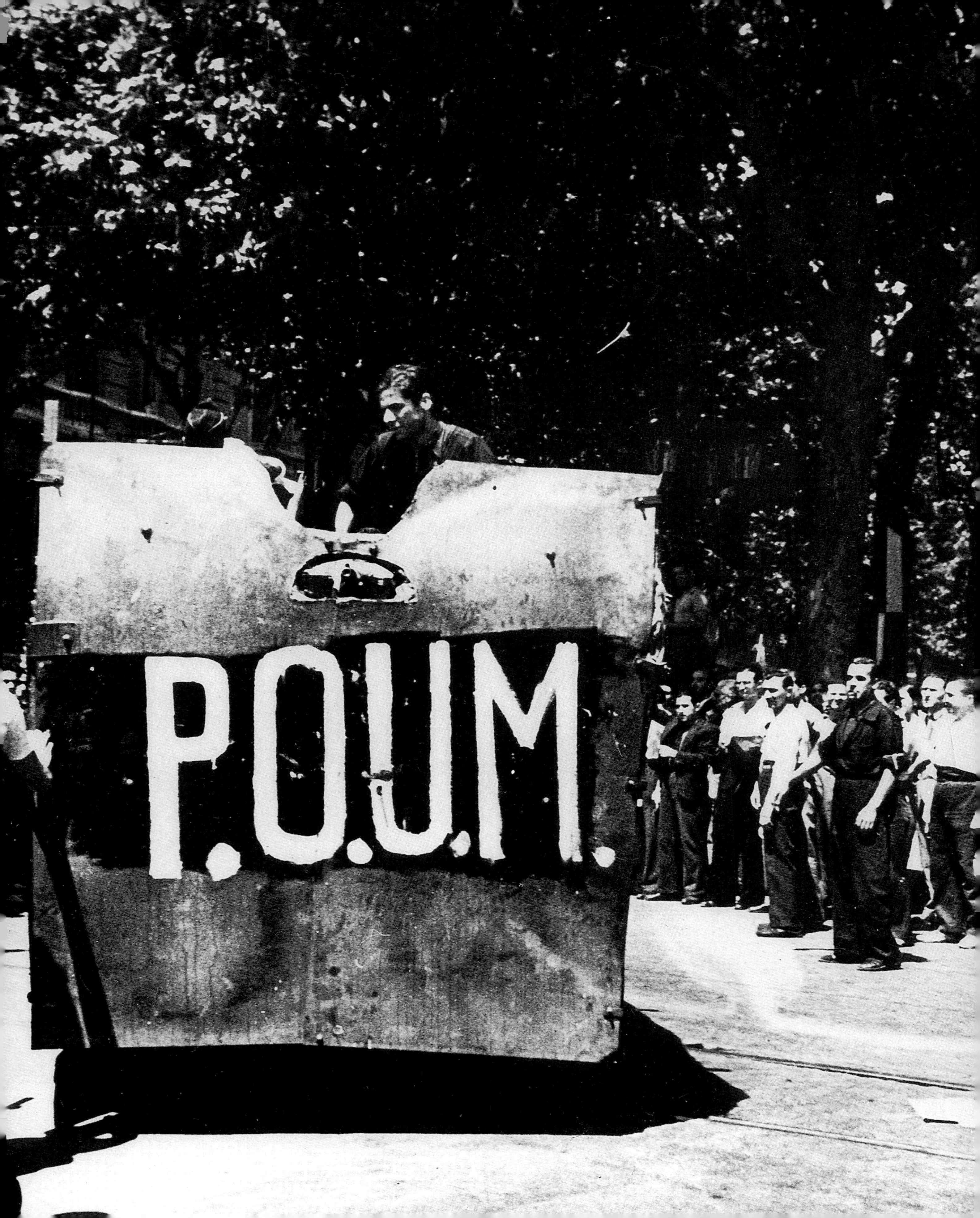
P.O.U.M.

Stourwater revisited: the Seven Deadly Sins

ON HIS SECOND VISIT *to Sir Magnus Donners' moated and battlemented home in the autumn of 1938 Nicholas is less impressed than he had been before.*

'Look, the castle,' said Isobel. 'Nobody warned me it was made of cardboard.'

Cardboard was certainly the material of which walls and keep seemed to be built, as we rounded the final sweep of the drive, coming within sight of a large castellated pile, standing with absurd unreality against a background of oaks, tortured by their antiquity into elephantine and grotesque shapes. . . .

We found ourselves among those scenes in blue, yellow and crimson, the tapestries illustrating the Seven Deadly Sins which surrounded the dining-room, remembered so well from my earlier visit. Then, I had sat next to Jean Duport. We had talked about the imagery of the incidents depicted in the tapestries.

That all seemed so long ago. I glanced round the room. If the rest of Stourwater had proved disappointing – certainly less overpowering in ornate magnificence – these fantastic tapestries, on the other hand, had gained in magnitude. More gorgeous, more extravagant than ever, they engulfed my imagination again in their enchanting colours, grotesque episodes, symbolic moods. . . . *'Luxuria' is still as impressive as ever,* a winged and horned female figure, crowned with roses, holding between finger and thumb one of her plump, naked breasts, while she gazed into a looking-glass, held up on one side by Cupid and on the other by a goat of unreliable aspect. The four-footed beast of the Apocalypse with his seven dragon-heads dragged her triumphal car, which was of great splendour.

After dinner Sir Magnus, who has taken up photography as a hobby, proposes that his guests – Nicholas and Isobel, Peter Templer and his second wife Betty, Hugh Moreland and Matilda and Sir Magnus's current mistress, Anne Umfraville – should themselves pose as tableaux of the Seven Deadly Sins.

And so, in an elaborate session, each guest assumes the character of a sin, with appropriate props, and is photographed by Sir Magnus. Here before us was displayed the nursery and playroom life of generations of 'great houses': the abounding physical vitality of big aristocratic families, their absolute disregard for personal dignity in uninhibited delight in 'dressing up', that passionate return to childhood, never released so fully in any other country, or, even in this country, so completely by any other class. *This sort of charade now seems archetypically 'thirties', and is reflected very closely in the elegant drawings of George Barbier.*

When, many years later, after Donners' death, Matilda rediscovers the photographs and shows them to Nicholas and Isobel, they seem like 'documents from a bygone age'.

TVRGIDA VENTOSOS IMITATA SVPERBIA FC
PASCITVR AERIO COPRVS INANE NOT

L'Orgueil

Childhood recalled

ON THE EVE OF THE SECOND WORLD WAR, *Nicholas's mind goes back to the summer of 1914, when he was living in his parents' house near Aldershot, a red-tiled bungalow called Stonehurst.* It had been built only thirteen or fourteen years before – about 1900, in fact – by some retired soldier, anxious to preserve in his final seclusion tangible reminder of service in India, at the same time requiring nothing of architecture likely to hint too disturbingly of the exotic splendours of Eastern fable. . . .

Stonehurst, as I have said, was a 'furnished' house, the furniture, together with pictures, carpets, curtains, all distinctly on the seedy side, all part of the former home of people not much interested in what the rooms they lived in looked like. However, India, one way and another, provided a recurrent theme that gave a certain cohesion to an otherwise undistinguished, even anarchic style of decoration. In the hall, the brass gong was suspended from the horn or tusk of some animal. . . . in the drawing-room, the piano was covered with a Kashmir shawl of some size and fine texture, upon which, in silver frames, photographs of the former owner of Stonehurst (wearing a pith helmet surmounted with a spike) and his family (flanked by Indian servants) had stood before being stowed away in a drawer. . . .

The house, built at the summit of a steep hill, was reached by a stony road – the uneven, treacherous surface

of pebbles probably accounting for the name – which turned at a right-angle halfway up the slope, running between a waste of gorse and bracken, from out of which emerged an occasional ivy-strangled holly tree or withered fir: landscape of seemingly purposeful irresponsibility, intentional rejection of all scenic design. . . .

The Stonehurst household consists of the family and the servants: Albert, the cook (later landlord of the Bellevue, see p. 99); Billson, Mrs Jenkins's highly strung maid; Bracey, Captain Jenkins's batman; Edith, the nurse; and Mercy, the housemaid – a self-contained, inbred, rather neurotic community. The day when all their tensions – domestic, psychological, religious – boil over is an ominous one, not only for the Jenkins family.

Not far away from Stonehurst lives the enigmatic figure of Dr Trelawney, the first of those disturbingly psychic characters who will crop up in Nicholas's life. Nicholas meets him from time to time on the heath, dressed up in patriarchal robes and followed by his disciples.

Dr Trelawney conducted a centre for his own peculiar religious, philosophical – some said magical – tenets, a cult of which he was high priest, if not actually messiah. This establishment was one of those fairly common strongholds of unsorted ideas that played such a part in the decade ended by the war. Simple-lifers, utopian socialists, spiritualists, occultists, theosophists, quietists, pacifists, futurists, cubists, zealots of all sorts in their approach to life and art, later to be relentlessly classified into their respective religious, political, aesthetic or psychological categories, were then thought of by the unenlightened as scarcely distinguishable one from another: a collection of visionaries who hoped to build a New Heaven and a New Earth through the agency of their particular crackpot activities, sinister or comic, according to the way you looked at such things.

'I thought it was the end of the world'

JUNE 28, 1914: *General Conyers and his wife have been invited to lunch; Uncle Giles has announced that he also is paying a visit, uninvited.*

The General and his wife were coming to Stonehurst after staying with one of Mrs Conyers's sisters, whose husband commanded a Lancer regiment in the area. Rather adventurously for that period, they were undertaking the journey by motorcar, a vehicle recently acquired by the General, which he drove himself. Indeed, the object of the visit was largely to display this machine, to compare it with the car my father had himself bought only a few months before. There was a good deal of excitement at the prospect of seeing a friend's 'motor', although I think my father a little resented the fact that a man so much older than himself should be equally prepared to face such grave risks, physical and financial.

At about one o'clock a car began painfully to climb the lower slopes of the hill. It could only contain General and Mrs Conyers. This was an unexpected excitement. I watched their slow ascent, which was jerky, like the upward movement of a funicular, but, contrary to my father's gloomy forecast, the steep incline was negotiated without undue difficulty. I was even able to open the Stonehurst gate to admit the vehicle. There could be no doubt now of the identity of driver and passenger. By that period, of course, motorists no longer wore the peaked cap and goggles of their pioneering days, but, all the same, the General's long check ulster and deerstalker seemed assumed to some extent ritualistically.

Lunch over, the party move to the drawing room, and it is here that the event occurs that made Mrs Jenkins think the world had ended. Billson, the maid, driven by various private stresses, decides to give notice. The door of the drawing room opened quietly. Billson stood on the threshold for a split second. Then she entered the room. She was naked.

General Conyers, accustomed to keeping his head in tight corners, deals with the situation. He picks up a Kashmir shawl, wraps it round Billson and leads her gently from the room.

'I thought it was the end of the world,' my mother said. I do not know to what extent she intended this phrase, so far as her own amazement was concerned, to be taken literally. My mother's transcendental beliefs were direct, yet imaginative, practical, though possessing the simplicity of complete acceptance. She may have meant to imply, no more, no less, that for a second of time she herself truly believed the Last Trump (unheard in the drawing-room) had sounded in the kitchen, instantly metamorphosing Billson into one of those figures – risen from the tomb, given up by the sea, swept in from the ends of the earth – depicted in primitive paintings of the Day of Judgement. If, indeed, my mother thought that, she must also have supposed some awful, cataclysmic division from on High just to have taken place, violently separating Sheep from Goats, depriving Billson of her raiment.

Later in the afternoon Uncle Giles arrives with fateful tidings. 'Some royalty in a motor-car have been involved in a nasty affair today. Heard the news in Aldershot. Fellow I went to see was told on the telephone. Amazing, isn't it, hearing so soon. They've just assassinated an Austrian archduke down in Bosnia. Did it today. Only happened a few hours ago.'

Uncle Giles muttered, almost whispered these facts, speaking as if he were talking to himself, not at all in the voice of a man announcing to the world in general the close of an epoch; the outbreak of Armageddon; the birth of a new, uneasy age. He did not look in the least like the harbinger of the Furies.

'Franz-Ferdinand?' asked General Conyers sharply.
'And his morganatic wife. Shot 'em both.'
'When did you say this happened?'
'This afternoon.'
'And they're both dead?'
'Both of them.'
'There will be trouble about this,' said the General.
Mrs Jenkins's words were indeed more than a figure of speech.

98

UNCLE GILES *had been a thorn in the flesh of the Jenkins family for as long as Nicholas could remember. Even his death comes at an inconvenient time, in the summer of 1939, when everyone is preoccupied by the coming war.*

Uncle Giles had been staying at the Bellevue, a seaside hotel kept by Albert, an old Jenkins retainer. Its general atmosphere reminds Nicholas of the Ufford, as if the Ufford itself had at last shipped anchor and floated on the sluggish Bayswater tide to this quiet roadstead. . . . Here, at any rate, Uncle Giles had died. By the summer sea, death had claimed him, in one of his own palaces, amongst his own people, the proud, anonymous, secretive race that dwell in residential hotels.

Nicholas has the task of sorting through Uncle Giles's possessions. Under the bed, he finds a Gladstone bag, a large example of its kind, infinitely ancient, perhaps the very one with which Uncle Giles had arrived at Stonehurst on the day of the Archduke's assassination. . . .

At first examination the Gladstone bag appeared to be filled with nothing but company reports. I began to go through the papers. Endless financial projects were adumbrated; gratifying prospects; inevitable losses; hopeful figures, in spite of past disappointments. The whole panorama of the money-market lay before one – as it must once have burgeoned under the eyes of Uncle Giles – like the kingdoms of the world and the glory of them. Hardly a venture quoted on the Stock Exchange seemed omitted; several that were not. There were two or three share certificates marked 'valueless' that might have been stock from the South Sea Bubble. Uncle Giles's financial investigations had been extensive. Then a smaller envelope turned out to be something different. One of the sheets of paper contained there showed a circle with figures and symbols noted within its circumference. It was a horoscope, presumably that of Uncle Giles himself.

He had been born under Aries – the Ram – making him ambitious, impulsive, often irritable. He had secret enemies, because Saturn was in the Twelfth House. I remembered Mrs Erdleigh remarking that handicap when I met her with Uncle Giles at the Ufford. Mars and Venus were in bad aspect as far as dealings with money were concerned. . . . The whole question of Uncle Giles's money affairs was a mysterious one, far more mysterious than anything revealed about him astrologically.

Ancestral voices prophesying war

DR TRELAWNEY, *together with Mrs Erdleigh and 'Scorpio' Murtlock, whom we shall meet later, represents a deeper and darker strain, at odds with the prevailing rationalism and materialism of the main story. Jenkins's attitude to all three is ambiguous. On the one hand, he sees them as figures of fun, whose weird beliefs, mystical pretensions and enigmatic pronouncements can be dismissed with patronising amusement. On the other hand, they disturb him. Trelawney is at various times compared to both Rasputin and Nostradamus.* 'There was something decidedly unpleasant about him, sinister, at the same time absurd . . . [a] combination of the ludicrous and the alarming.'

While clearing up Uncle Giles's affairs, Nicholas encounters him unexpectedly in the seaside hotel where his uncle has died. Bob Duport, the coarse and slightly shady operator who married Jean Templer, happens to be there too, and attempts to make fun of his prophetic utterances. Duport's materialism contrasts with Trelawney's occultism.

'What do you think, Dr Trelawney?'

'What will be, must be.'

'Which means war, in my opinion,' said Duport.

'The sword of Mithras, who each year immolates the sacred bull, will ere long now flash from its scabbard.'

'You've said it.'

'The slayer of Osiris once again demands his grievous tribute of blood. The Angel of Death will ride the storm. . . . The Four Horsemen are at the gate. The Kaiser went to war for shame of his withered arm. Hitler will go to war because at official receptions the tails of his evening coat sweep the floor like a clown's.'

'Seems an inadequate reason', said Duport.

'Such things are a paradox to the uninstructed – to the adept they are as clear as morning light.'

'I must be one of the uninstructed', said Duport.

'You are not alone in that.'

By one of those thematic echoes which make up the Dance to the Music of Time, Dr Trelawney's prophecy of the Second World War recalls the same moment of the First, when Uncle Giles brings news of Sarajevo.

The war: 'another stage of life'

O N THE MORNING *of Uncle Giles's funeral, Nicholas comes down to breakfast at the Bellevue and finds Bob Duport already there with the newspapers.*

'Nice news,' he said, 'isn't it?'

'What?'

'Germany and Russia.'

'What have they done? I haven't seen a paper.'

'Signed a Non-Aggression Pact with each other.'

He handed me one of the newspapers. I glanced at the headlines. . . . I felt a sinking inside me as I read. . . .

'It will be war all right now.'

When war does come, its first effect is one of oppressive calm: a tense, infinitely uneasy over-all stagnation imposed itself upon an equally uncomfortable, equally febrile over-all activity. Everybody was on the move. The last place to find a friend or relation was the spot where he or she had lived or worked in peacetime.

Nicholas concentrates his efforts on getting into the army, though he is already about thirty-five. But even his father, retired Lieutenant Colonel, has hopes of serving in some capacity. He was by this time totally immersed in the problem of how to bring about his own re-employment. . . . His days were spent writing letters to contemporaries who had achieved senior rank, hanging about his club trying to buttonhole them in person.

'I managed to have a word with Fat Boy Gort at the Rag yesterday,' he would say, speaking as if in a dream. 'Of course, I knew he could do nothing for me himself in his exalted position, but he wasn't at all discouraging.' *(Gort was Commander-in-Chief of the Army when war broke out, but was superseded after Dunkirk). Jenkins senior remains in unwilling retirement, but Nicholas manages to get a commission through the influence of Ted Jeavons's brother.* I went home through the gloom, exhilarated, at the same time rather afraid. Ahead lay the region beyond the white-currant bushes, where the wild country began, where armies for ever campaigned, where the Rules and Discipline of War prevailed. Another stage of life was passed, just as finally, just as irrevocably, as on that day when childhood had come so abruptly to an end at Stonehurst.

Castlemallock

T HE COMING OF THE SECOND WORLD WAR *meant an upheaval in Jenkins's life, as in that of most of his generation. Early in 1940 he finds himself as a junior officer joining his regiment in South Wales, near a town where his family had once owned property. It is a melancholy place, in keeping with his mood.* The cliffs below the site of the house, where all but foundations had been obliterated by the seasons, enclosed untidy banks of piled-up rock against which spent Atlantic waters ceaselessly dissolved, ceaselessly renewed steaming greenish spray.

After a week here the regiment is transferred to Castlemallock in Northern Ireland, a vast neo-gothic pile which had 'lain untenanted for twenty or thirty years before its requisitioning' by the army. In his 'rare, intoxicating moments of solitude,' Nicholas likes to sit in a window seat of the long gallery, 'reading Esmond, or watching the sun go down over the immense brick rampart of the walled garden.'

The castle's only literary association is with Lady Caroline Lamb, whose mother took her to Ireland in order to break off her affair with Lord Byron (this much is historical fact). A glade in the park was still known as 'Lady Caro's Dingle', and thought of a Byronic interlude here certainly added charm to grounds not greatly altered at the time of the rebuilding of the house. An air of thwarted passion could well be imagined to haunt these grass-grown paths, weedy lawns and ornamental pools, where moss-covered fountains no longer played. However, such memories were not in themselves sufficient to make the place an acceptable billet. At Castlemallock I knew despair. The proliferating responsibilities of an infantry officer, simple in themselves, yet if properly carried out, formidable in their minutiae, impose a strain in wartime even on those to whom they are a lifelong professional habit; the excruciating boredom of exclusively male society is particularly irksome in areas at once remote from war, yet oppressed by war conditions. Like a million others, I missed my wife, wearied of the officers and men around me, grew to loathe a post wanting even the consolation that one was required to be brave.

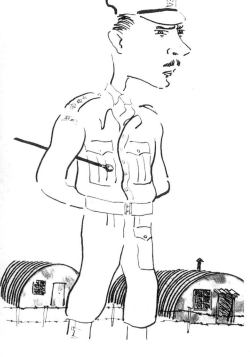

Rowland Gwatkin

CAPTAIN GWATKIN *is Jenkins's first company commander when he joins his regiment in Wales and remains in command during his sojourn in Northern Ireland.* [The] first sight of him revealed a novelty of character, at once apparent, though hard to define. There was, in the first place, some style about him. However much he might physically resemble the rest, something in his air and movements also showed a divergence from the humdrum routine of men. . . .

'What is your Christian name, Mr Jenkins?'

'Nicholas.'

'Mine is Rowland. The Commanding Officer says we should not be formal with each other off parade. We are brother officers – like a family, you see. So, when off duty, Rowland is what you should call me. I shall say Nicholas.'

Gwatkin is a serious and hard-working officer, dedicated to making his company the best in the battalion. But, as Nicholas gradually discovers, he is also a dreamer with romantic ambitions out of proportion to his ability. 'He just fancies himself as a great soldier', says another officer.

There was an air of resolve about him, the consciousness of playing a part to which a high destiny had summoned him. I suspected he saw himself . . . as an aspiring, restless spirit, who, released at last by war from the cramping bonds of life in a provincial town [*he had been in banking*], was about to cut a dashing military figure against a backcloth of Meissonier-like imagery of plume and breastplate, dragoons walking their horses through the wheat, grenadiers at ease in a tavern with girls bearing flagons of wine.

Gwatkin's dreams are destined to be shattered. First he is relieved of his Company after mismanaging a training exercise in which his troops get hopelessly behind schedule. His disappointment is temporarily softened by his love for Maureen, the local barmaid, with whom he has been conducting a somewhat inept courtship. But even this consolation is removed when he and Nicholas one evening find Maureen in the arms of one of the corporals. Gwatkin's military career comes to an inglorious end. Soon afterwards he is invalided out of the army and returns to the bank.

Tutelary deities

A SINGLE OIL LAMP threw a circle of dim light round the dining table of the farm parlour where we ate, leaving the rest of the room in heavy shadow, dramatising by its glow the central figures of the company present. Were they a group of conspirators – something like the Gunpowder Plot, for instance – depicted in the cross-hatchings of an old engraved illustration? It was not exactly that. At the same time the hard lights and shades gave the circle of heads an odd mysterious unity.

Army life for Nicholas always retains a touch of unreality. Cut off from normal existence, his mind tends to produce bizarre images and exotic parallels. He has already been struck by the resemblance of one of the colonels' faces to a bird – an angry, ageing bird, recently baulked of a field-mouse and looking about for another small animal to devour – *and that of the other to a dog*, a retriever, a faithful hound, sound in wind and limb, prepared to tackle a dog twice his size, or swim through a river in spate to collect his master's game, but at the same time not in the top class for picking up a difficult scent.

Now, watching them sitting on either side of the general, Nicholas has a new vision. All was manifest. Colonel Hogbourne-Johnson and Colonel Pedlar were animal-headed gods of Ancient Egypt. Colonel Hogbourne-Johnson was, of course, Horus, one of the sculptured representations in which the Lord of the Morning Sun resembles an owl rather than a falcon; a bad-tempered owl at that. Colonel Pedlar's dog's muzzle, on the other hand, was a milder than normal version of the jackal-faced Anubis, whose dominion over Tombs and the Dead did indeed fall within A & Q's province [*Adjutant and Quartermaster*]. Some of the others round about were less easy to place in the Egyptian pantheon. In fact, one came finally to the conclusion, none of them were gods at all, mere bondsmen of the temple.

In the blitz: April, 1941

A SINGLE NIGHT *brings death to some of Nicholas's closest friends. He meets Chips Lovell (now married to Isobel's sister Priscilla) at the Café Royal.* The tables and banquettes of the large tasteless room looked unfamiliar occupied by figures in uniform. . . . Lovell did not arrive until nearly half-past seven. He wore captain's pips.

Lovell confides that his wife is having an affair with Odo Stevens, a wartime acquaintance of Nicholas, who had actually introduced them. He departs for the Café Madrid, where the society hostess Bijou Ardglass is giving a fortieth birthday party; here he hopes to meet Priscilla and patch up his marriage.

Later in the evening, Nicholas learns what has happened at the Madrid. The narrator is Max Pilgrim, a cabaret singer and pianist who had been performing there.

'The Madrid is no more,' he said.
'Finished?'
'Finished.'
'The season or just your act?'
'The place – the building – the tables and chairs – the dance-floor – the walls – the ceiling – all those gold pillars. A bomb hit the Madrid full pitch this evening.'

Gradually the whole story comes out.

'Anybody killed?'

Pilgrim nodded.

'Many?'

Pilgrim nodded again.

'Helped to get some of them out,' he said.

'There were a lot?'

'Of course it's a ghastly muddle on these occasions', he said. 'Frenzied. Like Dante's Inferno. All in the black out too. The wardens and I carried out six or seven at least. Must have. They'd all had it. . . . I'm afraid it was Bijou's last party.'

Chips Lovell is among the dead. Nicholas goes that same evening to Lady Molly's, where Priscilla has been staying, to break the news, only to find that house too smouldering and wrecked by a bomb. Both Lady Molly and Priscilla have been killed.

The pressures of war

Jenkins's *battlefields are those of the military bureaucracy —
committees, desks, offices, telephones. It is a dark,
underground world, tense with anxiety and effort, which
(characteristically) makes him think of Wagner's
Nibelheim. The officer in charge of signals is* a near-midget,
middle-aged and two-pipped, with long arms and short
legs attached to a squat frame. . . . As he had hurried
fretfully down the long dark passages, apportioning hot
news to swell the in-trays at break of day, he seemed one
of the throng from the Goblin Market. Now, opening the
door of their room, identification was more precise. The
curtain had obviously just risen on the third drama of *The
Ring* — Mime at his forge — the wizened lieutenant
revealed in his shirtsleeves, crouched over a table, while
he scoured away at some object in an absolute fever of
energy.

'Good morning'.

There was no concealing a certain peevishness at
interruption of the performance at such a crucial
juncture, only a matter of seconds before the burst of
guttural tenor notes opened the introductory lament:

'Labour unending
Toil without fruit!
The strongest sword
That ever I forged . . .'

However, he discontinued his thankless task for a brief
space, though still clutching the polishing cloth in claw-
like fingers. It was not, in fact, Siegfried's sword to which
he was devoting so much attention . . . . but that by now
almost universally adopted – possibly Moghul –
contribution to military tailoring, the Sam Browne belt,
doubtless his own, the unbuckled brace of which waited
treatment on another table.

*Twice Nicholas's duties take him to the Cabinet offices, a series
of bomb-proof rooms underneath the government buildings in*

Whitehall, *where Churchill mostly lived and where the key decisions of the war were taken.* I followed the marine down flight after flight of stairs. It was like the lower depths of our own building, though more spacious, less shabby. . . . It was impossible to remain unaware of an atmosphere of exceedingly high pressure in this place, something much more concentrated, more intense, than that with which one was normally surrounded. This was not because work was unplentiful or disregarded in our own building; nor – some of it – lacking in immediacy or drama. However much those characteristics might there obtain, this ethos was something rather different. In this brightly lit dungeon lurked a sense that no one could spare a word, not a syllable, far less gesture, not of direct value in implementing the matter in hand. The power principle could almost be felt here, humming and vibrating like the drummings on the teleprinter. The sensation that resulted was oppressive, even a shade alarming.

This sense of urgent energy is focussed for Nicholas in the figure of the Chief of Imperial General Staff, Field Marshal Alanbrooke (seen here between Admiral Cunningham and Marshal Portal), whom he sees getting out of a car in Whitehall – a thickset general, obviously of high rank, wearing enormous horn-rimmed spectacles. He had just burst from a flagged staff car almost before it had drawn up by the kerb. Now he tore up the steps of the building at the charge, exploding through the inner door into the hall. An extraordinary current of physical energy, almost of electricity, suddenly pervaded the place. I could feel it stabbing through me. This was the CIGS.

Even Vavassor, the porter, the usually phlegmatic 'attendant spirit' to Nicholas's section, 'in a blue frock coat with scarlet facings and top hat with gold band', is impressed. Vavassor, momentarily overawed – there could be no doubt of that – came to attention and saluted with much more empressement than usual.

Allied liaison

B Y THE SPRING OF *1942, Jenkins has left his regiment and taken up duties in Whitehall as a liaison officer with the Polish forces in Britain. The Poles, under General Sikorski, are one of several national groups continuing the fight against Germany in exile, each needing careful diplomatic handling.* The rest of the section were concerned either with the original Allies – Belgium, the Netherlands, Luxembourg, Norway, Czechoslovakia – or Neutrals – some of whom from time to time were metamorphosed into Allies or enemies – running to nearly twenty in number.

At a meeting chaired by Widmerpool, now a major, the position of Sikorski in relation to other Polish leaders is discussed. [Widmerpool] had evidently read the subject up, at least familiarized himself with its salient points. Probably the knowledge was fairly thorough, as his capacity for work was enormous.

Relations with the Poles are at a particularly delicate point owing to the recent discovery by the Germans of the mass graves at Katyn, in which up to 10,000 Polish officers apparently murdered by the Russians in 1939, had been buried. To the British the whole episode is an embarrassment, since they have to maintain good relations with the Russians. Widmerpool typically has no time for moral judgements and sees the situation entirely from the point of view of expediency:

'Whatever materializes, even if it does transpire – which I sincerely trust it will not – that the Russians behaved in such a very regrettable manner, how can this country possibly raise official objection, in the interests of a few thousand Polish exiles, who, however worthy their cause, cannot properly handle their diplomatic relations, even with fellow Slavs. It must be confessed also, that the Poles themselves are in a position to offer only a very modest contribution, when it comes to the question of manpower. How, as I say, can we approach our second most powerful Ally about something which, if a fact, cannot be put right, and is almost certainly, from what one knows of them, the consequence of administrative inadequacy, rather than the wilful indifference to human life and the dictates of compassion? What we have to do is not to waste time and energy in considering the relative injustices war brings in its train, but to make sure we are going to win it.'

M. HUBERT PIERLOT

QUEEN WILHELMINA

Dr. BENES

KING HAAKON

GENERAL DE GAULLE

GENERAL SIKORSKI

KING GEORGE of the HELLENES Grand Duchess of LUXEMBOURG

KING PETER

LEADERS OF THE ALLIED NATIONS WHOSE HEADQUARTERS ARE IN BRITAIN

PRINTED IN ENGLAND

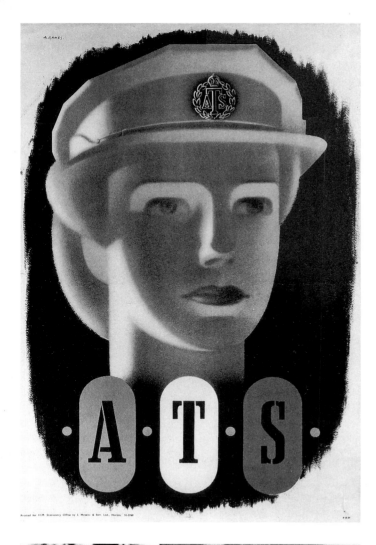

Pamela

Nicholas *first comes across Pamela Flitton in 1942, when he is working in Whitehall with Allied Liaison and she is an ATS driver.* Very young, she was one of those girls with a dead white complexion and black hair, the only colouring capable of rising above the boundlessly unbecoming hue of khaki. Instead of the usual ATS tunic imposed by some higher authority anxious that the Corps should look, if not as masculine as possible, at least as Sapphic, she had managed to provide herself, as some did, with soldier's battledress, paradoxically more adapted to the female figure.

As she drives him through London, Nicholas notes that she has the power of projecting around her a sense of vast resentment. . . . Her rankling animosity against the world in general was discharged with adamantine force. . . . Then, while driving through Hyde Park, she suddenly spoke of her own accord . . .

'You're Captain Jenkins, aren't you?'

'I am.'

'I think you know my mother.'

'What's your mother's name?'

'Flavia Wisebite – but I'm Pamela Flitton. My father was her first husband.'

This was Stringham's niece.

(Stringham's sister Flavia had married first Cosmo Flitton and then an American, Harrison F. Wisebite).

During the rest of the war, Nicholas hears frequent rumours of her promiscuous love life, and forms the view that what interests her in sexual adventures is the opportunity they give for making men (and women) suffer. Her beauty and her 'blend of frigidity with insatiable desire' will allow her to indulge these inclinations to the full.

After the war, in 1947, Nicholas visits her when she is living with the writer X. Trapnel, who is ill. He gave her one of those 'adoring looks' which Lermontov says mean so little to women. Pamela stared back at him with an expression of complete detachment. I thought of King Cophetua and the Beggar Maid, though Pamela was far from a pre-raphaelite type, or a maid, and, socially speaking, the boot was, if anything, on the other foot. No doubt it was Trapnel's beard. He had also allowed his hair to grow longer than usual. All the same, he sitting up on the divan, she standing above him, they somehow called up the picture.

I N THE SUMMER OF *1944 London is subjected to Hitler's latest secret weapon, the flying bomb. Deprived of sleep, Nicholas goes down to the ground floor of his block of flats. Here he encounters Pamela Flitton and Odo Stevens and – later – Mrs Erdleigh. As usual, Mrs Erdleigh's insights are uncannily close to the truth, and her diagnosis of Pamela's character will explain much that is to happen in the years to come. 'The girl herself is under Scorpio . . . and possesses many of the scorpion's cruellest traits . . . I fear she loves death and disaster . . .'. Odo Stevens introduces them.*

'My dear,' said Mrs Erdleigh, 'I well discern in your heart that need for bitter things that knows no assuagement, those yearnings for secrecy and tears that pursue without end, wherever you seek to fly them. No harm will come to you, even on this demonic night, that I can tell you. Nevertheless stay for a minute and talk with me. Death, it is true, surrounds your nativity, even though you yourself are not personally threatened – none of us is tonight. There are things I would like to ask you. The dark unfathomable lake over which you glide – you are under a watery sign and yet a fixed one – is sometimes dull and stagnant, sometimes, as now, angry and disturbed.' . . . Pamela held out her palm. . . . Mrs Erdleigh examined the lines. . . .

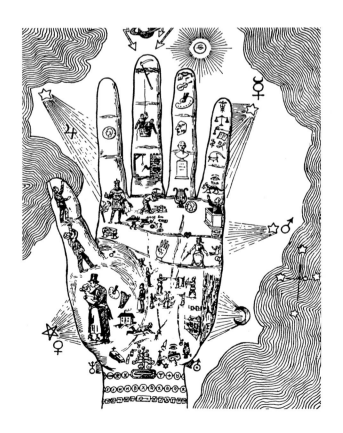

'. . . As I guessed, the Mount of Venus highly developed . . . and her Girdle . . . You must be careful, my dear . . . There are things here that surprise even me . . . *les tentations lubriques sont bien prononcées* . . . You have found plenty of people to love you . . . but no marriage at present . . . no . . . but perhaps in about a year . . .'

118

The vortex of becoming

'Who's it going to be?' asked Stevens. 'What sort of chap?'

'Mind your own business,' said Pamela.

'Perhaps it is my business.'

'Why should it be?'

'A man a little older than yourself,' said Mrs Erdleigh.

'A man in a good position.'

'Pamela's mad about the aged,' said Stevens. 'The balder the better.'

'I see this man as a jealous husband,' said Mrs Erdleigh. 'This older man I spoke of . . . but . . . as I said before, my dear, you must take good care . . . You are not always well governed in yourself . . . your palm makes me think of that passage in Desbarrolles, the terrible words of which always haunt my mind when I see their marks in a hand shown to me . . . *la débauche, l'effronterie, la licence, le dévergondage, la coquetterie, la vanité, l'esprit léger, l'inconstance, la paresse* . . . those are some of the things in your nature you must guard against, my dear.'

Whether or not this catalogue of human frailties was produced mainly in revenge for Pamela's earlier petulance was hard to know. Perhaps not at all. Mrs Erdleigh was probably speaking no more than the truth, voicing an analysis that did not require much occult skill to arrive at. In any case, she never minded what she said to anyone. Whatever her intention, the words had an immediate effect on Pamela herself, who snatched her hand away with a burst of furious laughter. It was the first time I had heard her laugh.

After Pamela has gone, Nicholas enquires after Dr Trelawney.

'He passed over not long after your uncle. Being well instructed in such enlightenments, he knew his own time was appointed – in war conditions some of his innermost needs had become hard to satisfy – so he was ready. Quite ready.'

'Where did he die?'

'There is no death in Nature' – she looked at me with her great misty eyes and I remembered Dr Trelawney himself using much the same words – 'only transition, blending, synthesis, mutation. He has re-entered the Vortex of Becoming.'

'I see.'

'But to answer your question in merely terrestrial terms, he re-embarked on his new journey from the little hotel where we last met.'

'Proustian musings' in Normandy

SOON AFTER THE INVASION OF FRANCE *Jenkins has the job of accompanying a group of Allied military attachés on a tour of the Normandy battlefield. Their first stop is at the seaside resort of Cabourg.* Wondering what the place was like in peacetime at the height of the season, I strolled to the side of the hotel facing the 'front'. On this façade, a section of the building – evidently the hotel's dining room, with half-a-dozen or more high arched windows – had been constructed so that it jutted out on to the esplanade. This promenade, running some feet above the beach, was no doubt closed to wheeled traffic in normal times. Now, it was completely deserted. The hotel, in café-au-lait stucco, with turrets and balconies, was about fifty or sixty years old, built at a time when the seaside was coming seriously into fashion.

And then – just as the party is moving out of town – he realizes that Cabourg was Proust's 'Balbec'. Scales fell from my eyes. Everything was transformed. . . . Through the high windows of the Grand Hotel's dining-room – conveying to those without the sensation of staring into an aquarium – was to be seen Saint-Loup, at the same table Bloch, mendaciously claiming acquaintance with the Swanns.

Proust is left behind, though 'Proustian musings still hung in the air when we came down to the edge of the water.' Here a strange, unearthly scene awaits them. In the foreground lay a kind of inland sea, or rather two huge lagoons, the further enclosed by moles and piers that seemed exterior and afloat; the inner and nearer, with fixed breakwaters formed of concrete blocks, from which, here and there, rose tall chimneys, rows of cranes, drawbridges. . . . 'Tiens', said General Philidor. 'C'est bien le Mulberry.'

The other two highlights of the trip for Jenkins are an encounter with men of his old regiment (including his friend Idwal Kedward, who has difficulty remembering him), and a meeting with 'the Field-Marshal'. The military attachés were led to a spot where a large map hung on a kind of easel.

'You'll want me to put you in the picture.'

With unexpectedly delicate movements of the hands, the Field-Marshal began to explain what had been happening. . . . One felt him essentially the kind of soldier Vigny had in mind when writing of the man who, like a monk, submitted himself to the military way of life, because he thought it right, rather than because it appealed to him.

'This day of general thanksgiving'

Aᴜɢᴜsᴛ *20, 1945. The war is over.* Summer . . . offered no warmth, but chilly, draughty, unwelcoming perspectives, under a grey and threatening sky. The London streets by this time were, in any case, far from cheerful: windows broken: paint peeling: jagged, ruined brickwork enclosing the shells of roofless houses. Areas of desolated buildings, the burnt and battered City, lay about St Paul's on all sides.

The Thanksgiving Service in St Paul's brings together the heads of Allied governments and their representatives for the last time, before the post-war world separates them. There is a sense of an era of history coming to an end, and an era in the lives of countless individuals who, like Jenkins, have been caught up in the events of history. There was an impression of capes and mitres, vestments of cream and gold, streaks of ruby-coloured velvet, the Lord Mayor bearing the City Sword point upward, khaki uniforms and blue, a train of royal personages . . . the King and Queen, the Princesses. . . .

'A great occasion'

SACRED TO THE MEMORY OF
LIEUTENANT-GENERAL SIR JOHN MOORE, K.B.

J ENKINS'S GROUP *of military attachés, for whom he is still responsible, are given places in the south transept of St Paul's. As the congregation gathers, he looks round the cathedral at the 'huge marble monuments in pseudo-classical style' which happen to be near.* I was delighted to find among them more than one of those celebrated in *The Ingoldsby Legends*, a favourite book of mine about the time we lived at Stonehurst. There, for example, only a few feet away from where the military attachés sat, several figures far larger than life were enacting a battle scene in which a general has been struck from the saddle by a cannon ball, as his charger bore him at a furious gallop across the path of a kilted private from some Highland regiment. There could be no doubt whatever this was:

'. . . Sir Ralph Abercrombie going to tumble
With a thump that alone were enough to dispatch him
If the Scotchman in front shouldn't happen to catch
          him.'

Stendhal had seen these monuments when he visited London.
'Style lourd,' he noted. 'Celui d'Abercrombie bien ridicule.'
Nevertheless, one felt glad it remained there. It put on record what was then officially felt about death in battle, begging all that large question of why the depiction of action in the graphic arts had fallen in our own day almost entirely into the hands of the Surrealists.
'La jolie figure de Moore rend son tombeau meilleur,' Stendhal thought.
This was against the wall by the side door through which we had entered the Cathedral, at right angles to the Abercrombie memorial. Less enormously vehement, this group too had its own exuberance of style, though in quite another mood. Here a sinister charade was being enacted by several figures not so gigantic in size. What they were doing was not immediately clear, until Barham's lines threw light on them too:

'Where the man and the Angel have got Sir John
          Moore,
And are quietly letting him down through the floor.'

Nicholas carefully arranges his mixed collection of Allied officers, some of whom, such as the Poles, had played a relatively prominent part in the war, but now found themselves deprived of their birthright for no reason except an unlucky turn of the wheel of international politics manipulated by the inexorable hand of Fate. *Is the ceremony of Thanksgiving itself, the 'Great Occasion', really only another 'sinister charade' like the monuments?*

'The best you could say for past love'

AFTER THE SERVICE *at St Paul's, Nicholas accompanies Colonel Flores, a South American diplomat, to his car and is introduced to his wife. It is Jean – rich, poised, still beautiful, amused to meet Nicholas again but not anxious to review the past. He and Isobel go to a party at her Knightsbridge flat.* Jean, rather superb in what was called 'The New Look' (another recent phrase), was dressed in a manner to which hardly any woman in this country, unless she possessed unusually powerful tentacles, could at that time aspire. She greeted us at the door. That she had become so fashionable had to be attributed, one supposed, to her husband. In the old days much of her charm – so it had seemed – had been to look like a well-turned-out schoolgirl, rather than an enchantress on the cover of a fashion magazine. The slight, inexpressibly slight, foreign intonation she had now acquired, or affected, went well with the splendours of *haute couture*.

He sees Jean once more, as a widow in her sixties. Somebody compares her to 'one of those sad Goya duchesses'.

The metamorphosis, begun when the late Colonel Flores had been his country's military attaché in London at the end of the war, was complete. She was now altogether transformed into a foreign lady of distinction. The phrase 'sad Goya duchess' did not at all overstate the case.

But the old intimacy has gone. Jean smiled graciously . . . There could have been no doubt in the mind of an onlooker that Jean and I had met before. That was about the best you could say for past love.

'The myriad forms of melancholy'

AFTER THE WAR, *Jenkins resumes his career by embarking on a biography of the seventeenth-century writer Robert Burton, author of 'The Anatomy of Melancholy'. To do his research he goes back to his old university.* Reverting to the university at forty, one immediately recaptured all the crushing melancholy of the undergraduate condition. As the train drew up at the platform, before the local climate had time to impair health, academic contacts disturb the spirit, a more imminent gloom was re-established, its sinewy grip in a flash making one young again. Depressive symptoms, menacing in all haunts of youth, were in any case easily aroused at this period, to be accepted as delayed action of the last six years. . . . As the days passed, the hypnotic pull to pay a call on Sillery grew increasingly strong, disinclination – that was, of course, far too strong a word, indeed not the right word at all – scarcely lessening, so much as the Sillery magnetism itself gathering force. . . . Sillery still retained his old rooms, receiving visitors willingly, even avidly, it was reported, with so far as possible the traditional elements of welcome.

He is now nearly eighty, and has recently been made a life peer. Sillery, moustache a shade more ragged and yellow, blue bow tie with white spots, more likely than ever to fall undone, was not much changed. Perhaps illusorily, his body and face had shrunk, physical contraction giving him a more simian look than formerly, though of no ordinary monkey; Brueghel's Antwerp apes. . . . so strong was this impression of metempsychosis that he seemed about to bound up onto the bookcases. . . .

'Ah, Burton?' said Sillery. 'An interesting old gentleman, I've no doubt. Many years since I looked into the *Anatomy*.'

But for Nicholas, the whole topic of Burton and his book is of more than academic, or indeed professional, interest. The title page showed not only Burton's own portrait in ruff and skull cap, but also figures illustrative of his theme; love-madness; hypochondriasis; religious melancholy. The emblems of jealousy and solitude were there too, together with those sovereign cures for melancholy and madness, borage and hellebore. Burton had long been a favourite of mine. A study of him would be a change from writing novels. The book was to be called *Borage and Hellebore.*

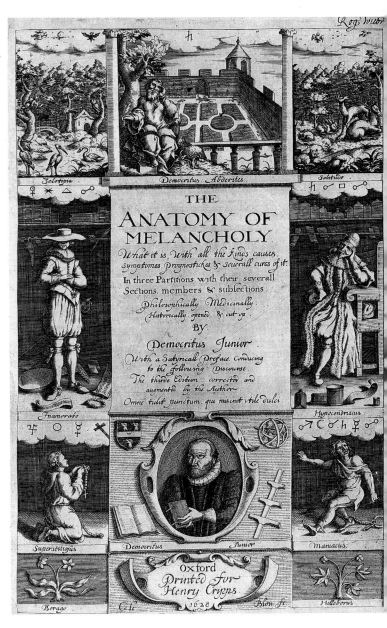

Melancholy is a leitmotif of the Dance. Nearly all the characters are in some way affected by it, and Nicholas likes to describe them according to Burton's, rather than any later psychologist's, diagnosis. At Erridge's funeral he muses: 'Melancholy was so often the explanation, anyway melancholy in Burton's term.' One of Widmerpool's deficiencies, perhaps, was that he lacked Melancholy, and the reason why he was attracted to Pamela was that she could supply it.

129

'This business of being a "Writer"'

X. TRAPNEL *(christened Francis Xavier, but he dropped the Francis) was loosely based on Julian Maclaren-Ross (photographed here in 1964). Like his real-life original, he is an egoist, a compulsive talker, making a precarious living by writing for periodicals but never successful enough to dispense with loans from his friends, though never without an attractive girlfriend. Trapnel, however, is not only a genuine writer but a man dedicated to literary perfection. Brilliant but unstable, he exists amid a circle of admiring pub-cronies, adopting a variety of theatrical roles. One of them is that of a spooky monster from a horror movie.* It turned out in due course that Trapnel's impersonations of Boris Karloff were to be taken as a signal that a late evening must be brought remorselessly to a close.

The turning-point in Trapnel's life comes when he falls in love with Pamela (now, inexplicably to Nicholas, married to Widmerpool). After a disastrous first introduction, he runs into Pamela again at a publisher's office: 'She behaved as if she quite liked me, but felt it would be wrong to show it. That was the moment when the thing hit me. I didn't know what to do. I felt quite ill with excitement. I mean both randy and sentimentally in love too. . . . Of course, I know I'm mad. I don't stand a chance. That's one of the reasons why the situation's nothing like Tessa – or any other girl I've ever been mixed up with. I admit it's not sane. I admit that from the start.'

Pamela, however, has marked him down. A few months later she is living with him in a seedy flat near Maida Vale, where Nicholas, visiting them, is reminded of King Cophetua and the Beggar Maid (see p. 116). Inevitably, she drains him of creativity and leaves him. When she does so, she takes with her the unfinished manuscript of his last novel and scatters it in the muddy waters of the Regent's Canal, where Trapnel finds its fragments, recognizing that it represents the end of his life: 'It's a sacrifice. One of those things you dedicate to the Gods. I remember reading about a sacred pool in an Indian temple, where good writing floated on the water, bad writing sank. Perhaps the Canal has the same property and Pam was right to put my book there.'

For Pamela's touch is mortal. Emotional warmth in her was directed only towards the dead, men who had played some part in her life, but were no more there to do so. That was how it looked. . . . It was Death she liked. *No image more vividly conjures up the white, haunting face of Pamela, in love with Death, than Alastair's Salome, clutching the severed head of John the Baptist, surrounded by the guards about to crush her with their shields.*

Conferring in Venice

IN THE SUMMER OF *1958 Nicholas attends an international writer's Conference in Venice, 'intellectuals from all over the world addressing each other on their favourite topics,' meeting some old friends and making new contacts, notably the formidable don Dr Emily Brightman. It is a brittle, academic milieu, but destined to be shaken by volcanic emotions. For there are other visitors to Venice beside those attending the Conference, and 'You've just got to sit in the Piazza long enough. You see everyone in the world if you do that.'*

One Sunday when the Conference is not in session Nicholas pays a visit to the elderly English ex-publisher and eccentric Daniel Tokenhouse, who gave him his first job and has retired to Venice to paint. Aggressively left-wing, ideological and 'primitive', Tokenhouse sees art as a means of propagating political doctrine. He is pleased to be compared to the Mexican painter Diego Rivera. 'I flatter myself in these experiments in style, now wholly abandoned, I have caught a small touch of Rivera's gift of speaking in a popular language.' *Typical subjects of Tokenhouse paintings are 'Four Priests Rigging a Miracle' and 'Any Complaints?', an army scene.*

The Conference coincides with the Venice Biennale, and Tokenhouse goes with Nicholas to show him round. 'I can guarantee,' *he tells him*, 'that the only sanctuary from subjectless bric-à-brac here will be in the national pavilions of what you no doubt term the Iron Curtain countries. We will visit the USSR first.'

The white pinnacled kiosk-like architecture of a small building, no doubt dating from pre-Revolutionary times, seemed by its outwardly church-like style to renew the ecclesiological atmosphere that pursued Tokenhouse throughout life. Within, total embargo on aesthetic abstraction proved his forecast correct. We loitered for a while over Black Sea mutineers and tractor-driving peasants.

They go on to explore the other 'national selections on view', abstract works which provoke Tokenhouse's derision. 'Absurd,' he keeps muttering. 'Preposterous.' In the French pavilion they meet two other colleagues from the Conference, Ada Leintwardine and Louis Glober, arguing over whether a certain sculpture shows 'African overtones influenced by Ernst' or is 'redolent of Samurai armour designed by Schwitters'.

Louis Glober is an American publisher and film-maker, a man of the world with wide interests and serviceable charm. Intrigued by Tokenhouse as a human type, he goes back with him to his studio and actually buys a picture – the second that Tokenhouse has ever sold. Nicholas has known Glober in former days, when he was said to have the look of a 'young Byzantine emperor'. His quietly forceful manner suggested a right to command, inexhaustible funds of stored up energy, overwhelming sophistication, limitless financial resource. At that age I did not notice a hard core of melancholy lurking beneath these assets.

Myths, modern and ancient

PAMELA *is staying in Venice too, much to the delight of the American scholar Russell Gwinnett, who is writing a book about X. Trapnel and hopes to learn from her. They establish an immediate and (to Nicholas rather unexpected) rapport.*

The three of us set off together. Nothing much was said until we were quite close to the hotel. Then, on a little humped bridge crossing a narrow waterway, Pamela stopped. She went to the parapet of the bridge, leant over it, looking down towards the canal. Gwinnett and I stopped too. She stared at the water for some time without saying anything. Then she spoke in her low unaccentuated manner.

'I've thought of nothing but X since I've been in Venice. I see that manuscript of his floating away on every canal. You know Louis Glober wants to do it as a film, with just that ending. It might have happened here. This place just below. . . . I threw the book away because it wasn't worthy of X. . . . X himself knew it was a necessary sacrifice. . . . You don't know what sacrifice is.'

Gwinnett gave an odd smile at that.

'What makes you think so?' . . .

'I'll show you.'

She slipped from off her shoulder the bag Glober had given her, wound the chain quickly about it, forming a rough knot. Then, holding the shortened links of gold, whirled round the bundle in the air, like a sort of prayer-wheel, and tossed it over the side of the bridge. There was the gentlest of splashes. The crocodile-skin (returned to its natural element) bobbed about for a second or two on the surface of the water, the moonlight glinting on metal clasps, a moment later, weighed down by the weight of its chain, sinking into the dark currents of the little canal. Gwinnett still did not speak. Pamela returned from the parapet from which she had watched the bag disappear.

Even more pointed is the visit of the Conference party to a Venetian palace to see a Tiepolo ceiling featuring the story of Candaules and Gyges, thus expounded by Dr Brightman.

'Candaules was king of Lydia . . . Gyges his chief officer and personal friend. Candaules was always boasting to Gyges of the beauty of his wife. Finding him, as the King thought, insufficiently impressed, Candaules suggested that Gyges should conceal himself in their bedroom in such a manner that he had opportunity to see the Queen naked. Gyges made some demur at that, public nakedness being a state the Lydians considered particularly scandalous . . . but Candaules insisted, so he gave in, and was hidden in the royal bedchamber. Unfortunately for her husband, the Queen noticed the reluctant voyeur stealing away – we see her doing so above – and was understandably incensed. She sent for Gyges the following day, and presented him with two alternatives: either he could kill Candaules, and marry her *en secondes noces*, or – no doubt a simple undertaking in their respective circumstances at the Lydian court – she would arrange for Gyges himself to be done away with. . . Gyges chose the former course of action. His friend and sovereign, Candaules, was liquidated by him, he married the Queen, and ruled Lydia with credit for forty years.' *(Tiepolo might well have painted this subject, only he didn't; the illustration here is by Jacob Jordaens).*

The story fascinates Pamela, whose own sex life includes both voyeurism and necrophilia.

The Mozart party

IN THE SUMMER OF *1959 Nicholas and his wife attend a charity performance of 'The Seraglio', an occasion that brings together a number of figures from the past, many of whom have assumed new positions with new partners in the Dance.*

The hostess is Rosie Manasch, the 'lively, gleaming little Jewess', now married to Odo Stevens, a reasonably successful author. The Stevens house in Regent's Park, not large by the standards of Rosie's parents, though done up inside with a touch of the old Manasch resplendence, had room for a marquee to be built out on to a flat roof at the back to create an improvised auditorium.

The opera is a success (Chandler is 'mad about Osmin'), although Moreland suffers a collapse that foreshadows his death a few months later. But the evening ends with a dramatic confrontation between Widmerpool and Pamela in which the nightmare of their life together is made horribly clear.

'Things drawing to a close'

NOVEMBER, 1959. *Nicholas visits the dying Moreland in St Thomas's Hospital, opposite the Houses of Parliament. It is a touching and melancholy meeting.* That morning was the last time I saw Moreland. It was also the last time I had, with anyone, the sort of talk we used to have together. Things drawing to a close, even quite suddenly, was hardly a surprise. The look Moreland had was the one people take on when a stage has been reached quite different from just being ill.

Nicholas leaves the hospital. It happens to be the day of the annual vintage car rally. Drizzle was coming down fairly hard outside. I walked back over the bridge. Vintage cars still penetrated the traffic moving south. They advanced in small groups separated from each other by a few minutes. More exaggerated in style, some of the period costumes assumed by drivers and passengers recalled the deerstalker cap, check ulster, General Conyers had worn, when, on the eve of the 'first' war, he had mastered the hill leading to Stonehurst, in his fabled motor-car. I wondered if the Conyers car had survived, to become a collector's piece of incalculable value. . . . I paused to watch them by the statue of Boadicea – Budicca, one would name her, if speaking with Dr Brightman – in the chariot. . . . Below was inscribed the pay-off for the Romans.

> Regions Caesar never knew
> Thy posterity shall sway.

Whatever else might be thought of that observation, the Queen was obviously driving the ultimate in British vintage makes. A liability suddenly presented itself, bringing such musings sharply to a close, demanding rapid decisions. Widmerpool, approaching from right angles, was walking along the Embankment in the direction of Parliament. It might have been possible to avoid him by crossing quickly in front, because, as usual when alone, his mind seemed bent on a problem.

Widmerpool is indeed beset by problems. Although now a life peer, he has become involved in obscure scandals relating to Eastern Europe – contacts with Russian agents, illegal business deals, Stalinist sympathies. . . . These he has survived, only to have his private life shattered by another scandal – Pamela's death in bizarre and sinister circumstances. Rumours are circulating that, staying in a London hotel with her lover Russell Gwinnett, she took an overdose and died as part of a perverted necrophiliac ritual; in love, to the last, with Death.

Widmerpool begins a rambling, incoherent address to Nicholas. He showed outward mark of the stresses endured. His body was thinner, the flesh of his face hanging in sallow pouches. So deeply, so all envelopingly, was he dressed in black, that he looked almost ecclesiastical. . . . He sounded more than a little unhinged. . . . Without altering his tone, he changed the subject.

'The squalor – the squalor of that hotel.'

Traffic, beginning to slow up at the amber, came at last to a halt at red. Grinding noises provided exemption from need to produce an audible reply. Widmerpool showed no sign of expecting anything of the sort.

'The sheer ingratitude,' he said.

'I must be getting on. There's a lot to do. I want to get home before dark.'

He was never greatly interested in other people's doings. I added some platitude about the evenings drawing in. Widmerpool did not question the notation of the days. He turned to wait for the other lights to change, enabling him to proceed towards his destination. I crossed Whitehall swiftly. Another burst of vintage cars was advancing towards the bridge.

Widmerpool's conversion

L ORD WIDMERPOOL, *as he now is, has been elected chancellor of one of the universities. Jenkins watches the installation ceremony on television. It is 1968, the year of student revolt.*

They had just reached the foot of a flight of steps. In the background were buildings in a contemporary style of scholastic architecture. The persons composing the crocodile of dons and recipients of honorary degrees were preceded by a man in uniform bearing a mace. The cortège was making its way across an open space, shut in by what were probably lecture-halls. A fairly large crowd of students of both sexes, parents, friends, onlookers of one sort or another, stood on either side of the route, watching the ceremony. . . . Then Widmerpool came into sight. As he did so there was scarcely time to take in more of him than that he was wearing a mortar-board and gold brocaded robe, its train held up by a page.

Widmerpool, advancing towards the camera, had turned to say a word to this small boy, apparently complaining that the hinder part of his official dress was being borne in a manner inconvenient to its wearer, when the scene suddenly took on a new and startling aspect. What followed was acted out so quickly that only afterwards was it possible to disentangle specific incident from overall confusion. On different sides of the path, at two points, the watching crowd seemed to part. From each of these gaps figures of indeterminate sex briefly emerged, then withdrew themselves again. Some sort of scuffle arose. An object, perhaps two objects, shot up in the air. In the background a flimsy poster, inscribed with illegible words outlined in shaky capital letters, fluttered for a second in the air, hoisted on the end of a long pole, then appeared to collapse. All these things, flitting by too quickly to be taken into proper account, were accompanied by the sound of singing or chanting. By the time I had grasped the fact that some sort of demonstration was afoot, Widmerpool was no longer in sight.

The two assailants 'of indeterminate sex', who have thrown pots of paint at Widmerpool, turn out to be J. G. Quiggin's twin daughters, Amanda and Belinda. By one of those shifts in perspective that go with the Dance of Time, his daughters' flamboyant defiance of authority has become a source of intense irritation to the formerly radical Quiggin. Much more unpredictable, however, is Widmerpool's reaction. He is converted on the spot from respectable, though very left-wing, political views to complete sympathy with the sixties generation. It is the first step on the path that will end with his rejection of a conventional life-style altogether.

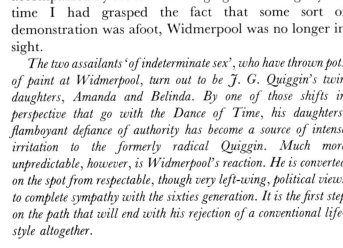

Secret harmony

Dr Trelawney *and his mystical movement are reborn in the cult led by 'Scorpio' Murtlock. The late sixties, however, are more sinister and more violent than the innocent days before World War I. Murtlock, whose real name is Leslie but who is known by his zodiac sign, is a young man of iron will and compelling strength of character.* His gestures were deft, ritualistic. He was totally in charge. This gift of authority, ability to handle people, was the characteristic attributed by hearsay. At first the outward trappings, suggesting no more than a contemporary romantic vagabondage, had put that reputation in doubt. Now one saw the truth of some at least of what had been reported of him. . . . There was an essentially un-sacerdotal side, one that suggested behaviour dubious, if not actively criminal.

When we meet Murtlock he and his companions are on the way to a prehistoric site near the Jenkins's house in the country, known as The Devil's Fingers.

'Why the name?'

'One Midsummer night, long ago, a girl and her lover were lying naked on the grass. The sight of the girl's body tempted the Devil. He put out his hand towards her. Owing to the night also being the Vigil of St John, the couple invoked the Saint, and just managed to escape. When the Devil tried to withdraw his hand, two of his fingers got caught in the outcrop of rock you find in these quarrying areas. There they remain in a petrified condition.'

Murtlock was silent. He seemed suddenly excited.

'Any other legends about the place?'

'The couple are sometimes seen dancing there. They were saved from the Devil, but purge their sin by eternal association with its scene.'

'They dance naked?'

'I presume.'

'On Midsummer Night?'

Two years later, at Midsummer 1970, Murtlock and his followers visit The Devil's Fingers again, and Nicholas hears reports of their having danced naked around a fire. By this time they include Widmerpool, who has moved from sympathizing with student revolution to becoming a drop-out himself. The object of the Midsummer rite was to summon up the dead Trelawney, but a quarrel develops between Widmerpool and Murtlock, and Widmerpool is seriously wounded. The figure who had always stood for the power of the will, meets a stronger will than his own, and – an elderly man – he submits totally to the hippy high-priest.

Widmerpool's end is bizarre. Murtlock orders him to run naked through the woods: 'Lord Widmerpool didn't object. He wanted to be in Harmony. He always wanted that. He took a moment to get properly awake. At first he could hardly stand, when he got up from the floor. All the same, he took his clothes off. . . . There was a warm mist. . . . He started to shout "I'm running, I'm running, I've got to keep it up". . . . It was rather a twisty way through the woods. Nobody could see him, especially in the mist, when they came round a corner, out of the trees, he was lying just in the road.'

'Collapsed?'

'Dead.'

Fifty years before, the schoolboy Widmerpool had emerged, running, from the mist. Now the Music of Time brings him, running in the mist, to the end of the Dance.

A Dance to the Music of Time consists of twelve novels, published over a period of twenty-five years, 1951–1975. They were published in the United Kingdom and Commonwealth by Heinemann in hardcover and by Fontana in paperback. In the USA they were published by Little Brown in hardcover and by Warner in paperback.

The historical period which they describe stretches from the eve of the First World War, 1914, to the Autumn of 1971. In this book the picture-spreads have been organized as far as possible to follow the sequence of events in the novels, though there are occasional overlaps. For those readers who wish to refer to particular episodes, we give here a list of the component novels and the pages of the present book which relate to them.

List of Illustrations

(Pictures are listed from top left to bottom right)

42–43 *St. Sebastian*, painting by Perugino
(c.1445–1523). The Louvre, Paris

View of the Rubens Gallery, Louvre,
painting by L. Béroud, c.1900. Photo
Roger-Viollet

Love in Autumn, painting by S. Solomon,
1866. Private Collection. Photo Courtesy
Sotheby's London

The Beheading of St John the Baptist,
painting by Puvis de Chavannes, 1869.
Barber Institute of Art, the University of
Birmingham

44–45 The Albert Memorial. Photo Edwin Smith

Kensington Gardens, painting by W.
Dobell, 1935

46–47 Staircase in Belgravia. Photo Westminster
City Libraries

The Hit, painting by F. Leighton, c.1893

Clothes and Car. Photo Cecil Beaton, 1927.
Courtesy of Sotheby's London

48–49 Dinner party, illustration by P. Mourgue,
Vogue, 1930. Copyright Condé Nast
Publications Ltd

Lady in harem, detail of *Rhamsès dans son
harem* by Lecomte du Noüy, 1885. Photo
Courtesy The Fine Art Society, London

King George V and Tsar Nicholas II in
torch dance at the wedding of Princess
Victoria Louise, 1913. *Illustrated London
News* Jubilee Number, 1935

Lady Haig's model for Haig Memorial.
Illustrated London News, 1929

Indian drawing a bow, statue by I. Mestroviç
(1883–1961). *Illustrated London News*, 1929

50–51 Debutantes, detail of drawing, *Tatler* 1929

Red Drawing Room, Dorchester House,
London. Photo H. Bedford-Lemere.
National Monuments Record, London

Dress by Louise Boulanger, 1927

Lady Barber, detail of painting, by J. J.
Shannon, 1912. The Barber Institute of
Fine Arts, The University of Birmingham

The Frog Footman, illustration by Tenniel
from *Alice's Adventures in Wonderland* by
Lewis Carroll, 1865

52–53 Detail based on *Selling the Daily Worker* by
C. Branson, 1937. Noreen Branson
Collection

The Quadriga, sculpture by A. Jones,
1912, Constitution Arch, Hyde Park
Corner. Photo by Ian Pleeth

J. Walker whisky advertisement by Doris
Zinkeisen, 1927

54–55 Café de Paris, detail of painting by Muriel
Minter, c.1930. Geffrye Museum, London

Portrait of a lady, detail of painting by
Kees van Dongen, 1925. Musée National
d'Art Moderne, Paris

Baby Wentworth and Bijou Ardglass,
cartoon by Osbert Lancaster

56–57 Homeward Way. Photo Bill Brandt, c.1934

Shepherd Market. Author's collection

Passers-by, detail of watercolour by R.
Schlichter, c.1926

'P died for Purity
and when I say that
I mean a green thought
through a green hat.'
Illustration by Edward Burra from *ABC
for the Theatre* by Humbert Wolfe, 1932
(alluding to Michael Arlen's novel *The
Green Hat*)

58–59 Entrance to Hever Castle.

Long Gallery, Hever Castle. Photo *Country
Life*

Lust, detail from The *Seven Deadly Sins*,
table panel by H. Bosch (1450–1516). The
Prado, Madrid

Staircase, Chirk Castle. Photo Christina
Gascoigne

60–61 *The Old Dealer*, two details of painting by
C. Spencelayh, 1925. Photo courtesy Richard Green Gallery, London

Bubbles, detail of print after painting by
Sir J. Millais, 1886. Photo Mansell Collection, London

For he had spoken lightly of a woman's name, print by John A. Lomax. Private collection

Olympia, detail of painting by E. Manet, 1863. Musée d'Orsay, Paris

Nude, detail of drawing by M. Beckmann, 1929

62–63 Prince's Square neighbourhood, Bayswater, painting by Noel Spencer. Museum of London

The Lounge, Grosvenor Hotel. Photo Bedford Lemere, National Monuments Record

Mrs. Erdleigh, cartoon by Mark Boxer, 1967

Five cards, from an originally French set of c.1830

64–65 Niche with sculpture, Palm Court, Ritz Hotel, London. Photo K. Collie

Dining in London, illustration in *Vogue*, 1934. Copyright Condé Nast Publications Ltd

Jantzen advertisement, Great West Road, London, c.1930. Photo Courtesy Jantzen Inc.

66–67 Queueing at the cinema in the 1930s. BBC Hulton Picture Library

Still from *Man of Aran*, 1934. Courtesy Rank Organisation

Poster for *Drums*, A. Korda film, 1938. Kobal Collection

Two stills from *Mädchen in Uniform*, 1932. National Film Archive

68–69 Woman smoking a hookah, detail of painting *Algerian Women in their Apartment* by E. Delacroix, 1834. Louvre, Paris

Le Chapeau de Paille, detail of painting by P. P. Rubens, c.1630. National Gallery, London

Rutland Gate. Photo Ian Pleeth

The Giantess, detail of painting by R. Magritte, 1931. Museum Ludwig, Cologne

70–71 *Charge on the Modder River*, illustration by St. Berkeley, 1903.

Noga's Cello, painting by A. Arikha, 1979. Private collection.

Gentleman at Arms, watercolour, 1924. Reproduced by Gracious permission of Her Majesty The Queen.

Mandala, produced by a female patient of C. Jung

72–73 House in South Kensington. Photo Ian Pleeth

Cocktails, drawing by F. Marshall from *London West*, 1944

The Doorway, painting by D. Wells (1881–1973)

74–75 Advertisement, 1937

Model wearing evening dress, *Vogue* 1934. Copyright Condé Nast Publications Ltd

Portrait of a lady, painting by Augustus John (1878–1961). National Museum of Wales, Cardiff

View in Surrey

French postcard, 1930s. Author's collection

76–77 Constant Lambert, portrait by Christopher Wood, 1926. National Portrait Gallery, London

Folly, detail from *Allegory of Time* by Bronzino (1503–72). National Gallery, London

Beethoven composing, detail of drawing by P. J. N. Geiger (1805–80)

78–79 Detail of *Selling the Daily Worker* by C. Branson, 1937. Noreen Branson Collection

Hunger March, Hyde Park, February 1934. Popperfoto, London

Woman's Day, Soviet poster by A. Strahov, 1922

80–81 Drawing room, Calke, Derbyshire. Photo National Trust

Boy's Own Paper, August 1929

Index

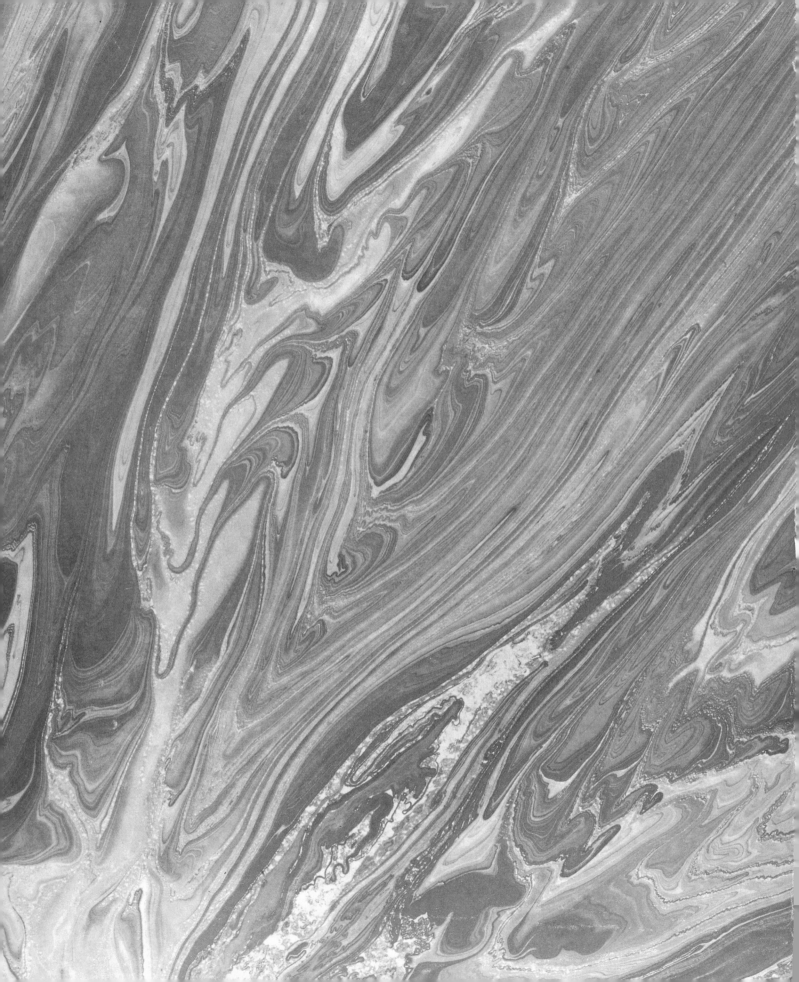